QUICK & EASY AIR FRYER COOKBOOK

100 Keto-Friendly Recipes to Cook in Your Air Fryer

Carolina Cartier, MSN

chartwell
books

Brimming with creative inspiration, how-to projects, and useful information to enrich your everyday life, Quarto Knows is a favorite destination for those pursuing their interests and passions. Visit our site and dig deeper with our books into your area of interest: Quarto Creates, Quarto Cooks, Quarto Homes, Quarto Lives, Quarto Drives, Quarto Explores, Quarto Gifts, or Quarto Kids.

First published in 2021 by Chartwell Books,
an imprint of The Quarto Group,
142 West 36th Street, 4th Floor,
New York, NY 10018 USA
T (212) 779-4972 F (212) 779-6058
www.QuartoKnows.com

Chartwell titles are also available at discount for retail, wholesale, promotional, and bulk purchase. For details, contact the Special Sales Manager by email at specialsales@quarto.com or by mail at The Quarto Group, Attn: Special Sales Manager, 100 Cummings Center Suite 265D, Beverly, MA 01915, USA.

Library of Congress Control Number: 2021936493

10 9 8 7 6 5 4 3 2 1

ISBN: 978-0-7858-3956-9

Publisher: Rage Kindelsperger
Creative Director: Laura Drew
Managing Editor: Cara Donaldson
Project Editor: Leeann Moreau
Editorial Assistant: Yashu Pericherla
Cover Design: Andrea Ho
Interior Design: Beth Middleworth

Printed in China

This book provides general information. It should not be relied upon as recommending or promoting any specific diagnosis or method of treatment for a particular condition, and it is not intended as a substitute for medical advice or for direct diagnosis and treatment of a medical condition by a qualified physician. Readers who have questions about a particular condition, possible treatments for that condition, or possible reactions from the condition or its treatment should consult a physician or other qualified healthcare professional.

CONTENTS

AN INTRODUCTION TO THE KETO DIET

WHAT IS KETO?

A ketogenic diet (also known as a keto diet) is a low-carbohydrate diet. The standard American diet has us eating a lot of carb-heavy, low-fiber fruits, starchy vegetables, and grains. On a keto diet, you lean instead toward foods high in fat, with a moderate amount of protein—meats, oils, nuts, and seeds—and low-carb vegetables and fruits.

Pre-keto, your body relied on carbohydrates as a main energy source. On a keto diet, your body has to turn on its fat-burning system. Without easy carbs to run on, the liver gets to work, turning stored fat into an alternative energy source called ketones.

And you guessed it: that's where the diet gets its name. Ketosis is the state of producing ketones, and producing ketones is what the body does when it's using fat as fuel.

WHY KETO?

Keto eaters and dieticians agree that keto's biggest benefit is relatively fast weight loss over a short period of time. People who eat a keto diet also report feeling more energetic, having more mental clarity, and being able to lose weight without feeling deprived of delicious, filling food.

Researchers are looking at other possible benefits of keto with great interest. Keto diets were used as early as the 1920s to help treat epilepsy in children. Some scientists believe keto also holds promise as a way to improve brain health, heart health, and blood sugar levels as well as to help people reach a healthy weight.

WHAT DO KETO DIETERS EAT?

All foods (and all diets) are built of the same three main components (called macronutrients): carbohydrates, proteins, and fats. Keto eating is about striking a very specific balance among those three components.

If you're like most Americans, your pre-keto diet relied on carbohydrates for most of its energy needs. The U.S. Department of Agriculture recommends a diet in which more than half of the calories come from carbohydrates, with fewer calories coming from fats and proteins. Their recommended breakdown of macronutrients looks like the chart at the right.

The keto diet flips these recommendations upside down. You eat some carbs and an adequate amount of protein, but most of your calories come from fat. There are several different versions of the keto diet, each recommending a slightly different ratio of macronutrients. Some of the commonly recommended micronutrient ranges are shown in the chart at the far right.

This macronutrient ratio—this combination of very few carbs, just enough protein, and as much fat as you need—is the defining characteristic of a keto diet.

WHY DOES IT WORK?

When carbs are plentiful, your body uses them first. When you eat carbs, your body easily turns them into glucose, and your pancreas cranks out a hormone called insulin to help carry that glucose to all the areas of your body that use glucose as fuel. By switching to a keto diet, you drastically change the balance of the *kinds* of nutrients available for your body's energy needs. This big change causes a correspondingly big shift in the way your body burns energy.

With fewer carbs coming in, the body first uses up glucose that's been stored in the liver. Then it turns, temporarily, to mining glucose from muscle tissue. That doesn't last long, though. After a few days, the body kicks into ketosis. The pancreas stops making so much insulin, and the liver ramps up its business of turning fat—the fat you've just eaten and the fat stored in the body—into ketones, packets of energy that, when released into the

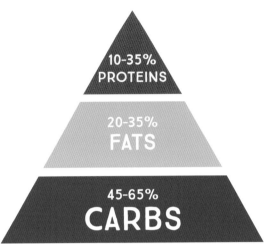

U.S. DEPARTMENT OF AGRICULTURE RECOMMENDATIONS

10-35%
PROTEINS

20-35%
FATS

45-65%
CARBS

THE KETO DIET RECOMMENDATIONS

5-10%
CARBS

15-30%
PROTEINS

60-80%
FATS

blood, are a perfect alternative fuel, keeping everything humming along just as glucose would—while burning existing fat rather than creating more.

Ketosis happens on a non-keto diet, as well; it just happens less frequently and for specific reasons, for example during periods of fasting (including overnight during sleep) and during intense exercise. But on the keto diet, you *stay* in ketosis—not by fasting or by running a marathon, but simply by not taking in enough carbs to cue your body to shift *out* of fat-burning mode.

More research is needed on exactly why keto dieters see good weight loss results. One theory is that the body has to use more calories to burn fat than it does to burn carbs. Another is that lower insulin makes it easier to lose fat and keep muscle.

Still another observation researchers are exploring is that many people simply feel less hungry on a keto diet. Why? It could be that fat, protein, and low-carb fruits and veggies are all foods that make a person feel fuller, longer (whether or not the person is in ketosis). Or it could be that ketosis's lower insulin levels (and lower amounts of other hormones that decrease when you eat fewer carbs) decrease the appetite. Another possibility is that the ketones themselves have a role in lowering hunger levels.

THE SHIFT INTO KETOSIS AND THE "KETO FLU"

In your first several days of keto eating, your body is using up sugars stored in your blood. You may start losing weight quickly right away (often due to loss of water and stored sugars). About four days into your keto journey, you'll likely notice some signals that you're reaching ketosis:

- lower appetite or fewer cravings
- change in the smell of your breath
- feeling tired, foggy, or sick
- low energy
- difficulty falling asleep
- constipation or diarrhea

Some of these aren't so pleasant! The tiredness, fogginess, and digestive issues are sometimes even known as the "keto flu." But don't worry; these symptoms are temporary. They're signs of your brain and body adjusting to the different diet.

It can take a few days or up to a month for everything to start running well with the new fuel. But these issues usually become less bothersome and fade away over a few days or weeks. And people who stick with the keto diet often feel sharper, sleep better, and have more steady energy than they did pre-keto.

ELECTROLYTES

One thing that may help ease the transition into ketosis: keeping an eye on your intake of electrolytes—meaning sodium, magnesium, and potassium. When you're first starting a keto diet, several factors may upset your usual electrolyte balance. If you ate a lot of processed, salty foods pre-keto, you're probably taking in much less salt now. Plus, during the transition to ketosis, your body loses a lot of water. This disturbance in your electrolyte intake may cause some of the "keto flu" symptoms, and restoring it may help resolve those symptoms. Stay hydrated, take supplements if needed, and make sure you include foods rich in electrolytes (avocados, nuts, and spinach and other dark leafy greens) in your diet.

KNOW YOUR NUTRITIONAL INFORMATION

To stay in ketosis, it's important to stick to the right balance of carbs, fats, and proteins. By limiting your carbs and protein, you keep your body in that fat-burning state. The exact percentage of calories needed from each nutrient is different for each body, depending on your age, gender, size, activity level, and even how far into your keto journey you are.

For your own recipes or other recipes you find online, you can use any of the following apps and websites to calculate your nutritional information. Keep in mind that not all apps are created equal, and the nutritional information will change based on the sources that each service references.

> ### RESOURCES FOR CALCULATING NUTRITIONAL INFORMATION
>
> WWW.CRONOMETER.COM
>
> WWW.KETODIETAPP.COM
>
> WWW.DIETDOCTOR.COM

As you figure out what works for your body, food labels—and recipes with nutritional information—are your friends. Here's the information you'll want to focus on:

THE BIG THREE: MACRONUTRIENTS

Every food—and, therefore, every diet—is made up of three main building blocks: carbohydrates, fats, and proteins. These are every body's three sources of energy (calories), and eating the right combination of these three macronutrients (sometimes called the macronutrient ratio) is the key to the keto diet. Every recipe in this book includes the nutrient values.

CARBOHYDRATES AND NET CARBS (5 TO 10 PERCENT OF YOUR DAILY CALORIES)

Carbohydrates, also known as carbs, include sugars, starches, and fibers. They're found in grains, dairy products, starchy vegetables, fruits, and of course soft drinks and any food that's sweetened with added sugar. Some keto dieters limit *all* carbs. Others limit only starches and sugars, eating fiber freely. The amount of carbs in a food minus the amount of fiber is known as the food's net carbs.

A big challenge of starting a keto diet is finding the right carbohydrate intake *for you*. Some keto experts recommend starting with a very low carb intake of about 20 grams of net carbs per day, and then increasing the number of carbs gradually (about 5 additional grams per day each week), regularly checking your ketone levels with a blood ketone meter (available in the $100 range) so you know whether you're still producing ketones. If your meter detects no ketones (or very few), it means you've exceeded your ideal carb intake for ketosis and it's time to cut back.

The ideal carb intake is different for each person, but a common upper limit is about 50 grams of total carbs (or 20 to 30 grams of net carbs) per day. You can choose to "spend" that daily carb allowance on rice, potatoes, or bread. But you'll find that, when it comes to grains and starchy vegetables, even 50 grams doesn't go very far. It amounts to about a cup of pasta or rice or half of a small bagel. The good news is that carbs are much tastier, more nutritious, and more filling when they're packed into natural, high-fiber foods such as berries, nuts, and non-starchy vegetables, including leafy greens, peppers, cauliflower, and just about any other veggie that grows above ground. To eat that same 50 grams of carbs, you can fill a heaping plate with berries or vegetables or a smaller bowl with nuts. You'll feel fuller *and* get more of the micronutrients you need.

Net carbs are calculated for each recipe by subtracting fiber from the carbohydrates.

PROTEIN (15 TO 30 PERCENT OF YOUR DAILY CALORIES)

Protein is found in meat, eggs, dairy products, nuts, and seeds. It's an essential macronutrient and important for maintaining healthy lean muscles, but to stay in ketosis it's important not to take in too much of it. If you take in excess protein, your body converts what you don't need into sugars, and your liver takes those sugars as a signal that it's okay to stop producing ketones—defeating the purpose of your low-carb eating.

You can use your current weight as a starting point to figure out your daily protein needs. Take your weight in pounds and multiply it by 0.6. The result is a good estimate of the *low* end of your daily protein needs (in grams). The upper end of that range—the maximum number of grams of protein you're likely to need—is simply your weight in pounds (that number of grams). Similarly, you can take your weight in kilograms and multiply it by 1.3 for the low end and 2.2 for the high end of your target protein range.

A couple of caveats go along with those guidelines. People who are very active generally need more protein to maintain their muscles, so make sure you account for that when deciding whether to aim for the low or high side of your target protein range. Also, people who have a high body fat percentage may come up with a better protein target by basing their calculations on lean body mass rather than on total body weight. Lean mass means body weight minus the weight that comes from fat. (A trainer or nutritionist can help find your body fat percentage and use it to calculate lean mass.)

Great keto-friendly sources of protein include all types of meat, fish, and eggs; soy products such as tempeh and tofu; and full-fat cheeses and yogurts.

FAT (60 TO 80 PERCENT OF YOUR DAILY CALORIES)

Every healthy diet includes fats; they keep countless body systems running well, and certain vitamins can't be absorbed in the body without them. But not all fats are created equal. Some come straight from a natural source; some are highly processed. And fats from different animal and plant sources have different benefits (and some have drawbacks).

MONOUNSATURATED AND POLYUNSATURATED FATS

These fats are liquid at room temperature. You'll find monounsaturated fats in olive and avocado oil, and in some nuts. Polyunsaturated fats are found in fish, walnuts, and several types of vegetable oils. Both types of unsaturated fats are known to have big benefits for cholesterol levels, heart health, and brain function, and most Americans don't get enough of them. The keto diet is a golden opportunity to enjoy these energy-packed delights.

SATURATED FATS

Saturated fats are naturally solid at room temperature. Butter, coconut oil, and fats from red meat all fall into this category.

Saturated fats are a controversial topic among health scientists. For many years, research suggested a clear link between these fats and heart disease. But more recent studies have shown the connection to be more complicated. Although some experts still suggest we should minimize our intake of saturated fats, others say that, for heart health, the *amount* of saturated fat we eat is less important than what we eat *alongside* saturated fat, or what we eat *instead* if we do reduce our saturated fat intake. Doctors and nutritionists who advocate for keto say it's important not just to think about the amount of saturated fat in the diet, but to consider other factors, such as:

- the source of the saturated fat
- which other nutrients are in the food
- where the food fits in your overall diet
- how *your* body responds
- the effect of *your* overall diet on *your* health

Taking all this into account, most keto diets—and the recipes in this book—include generous amounts of saturated fats from a variety of sources.

TRANS FATS

Also called partially hydrogenated fats, trans fats are vegetable fats that have been modified through an industrial process to make them solid at room temperature (for decades they were the main ingredient in margarine and shortening). They are so clearly linked to heart disease, diabetes, and other illnesses that their production has been banned in the United States since 2018, and the World Health Organization is working to eliminate them worldwide by 2023. You're unlikely to find foods containing trans fats on grocery store shelves, but if you do, steer clear.

CALORIES / ENERGY

One of the joys of a keto diet is that you usually *don't* need to keep track of calories. Of course, calories still matter. If you take in more energy than your body uses, you may gain weight, even on a keto diet. But many people find that the balance of foods on the keto diet is so satisfying, they're not inclined to eat more than they need.

Calories are listed on the top line of every U.S. nutrition label. The number of calories in a food is a measurement of how much energy that food provides. On food labels in the United States (and in the recipes in this book), the word *calories* is short for *kilocalories*.

In some countries, including the United Kingdom and throughout Europe, food labels give this same information a little differently. Instead of calories, the top category is called energy. European food labels list energy numbers in two different ways. The first, kilocalories (kcal), is exactly the same as what U.S. labels call *calories*. The second, kilojoules (kJ), is a different measurement system.

So, if in the United States a food is labeled *Calories: 100*, in Europe that very same food's label might say *Energy: 100kcal*. In Australia, it might say *418.4kJ*. They all measure the amount of energy in the food.

MICRONUTRIENTS

Micronutrients are the vitamins and minerals that our bodies need to work well and maintain health. Generally, our bodies need them in very small amounts. For example, while all diets include tens or hundreds of *grams* of protein, carbs, and fats each day, the amount of vitamin B we need each day is just a couple of *micrograms*.

Micronutrients don't provide energy (they don't have calories), but they're essential for good health. That's one reason it's important to eat a variety of foods, take supplements if necessary, and—especially if you're avoiding certain foods or food groups—get good nutritional advice from a doctor or other health professional to make sure you're taking in everything you need.

KNOW YOUR LOW-CARB SWEETENERS

Some recipes in this book call for sugar substitutes or for products (such as sugar-free ketchup and sugar-free chocolate chips) that may contain low-carb sweeteners. Choosing sweeteners can be complicated because not all sugar substitutes are low-carb, and some low-carb sweeteners can have the same negative impacts on your fat-burning state that sugar can (they can still spike your insulin and lead to weight gain).

The top three recommended keto-friendly sweeteners are:

- **Stevia.** Extracted from the leaves of a plant in the sunflower family, this sweetener is available in powder or liquid form. It has zero calories and won't raise your blood sugar levels. It is several hundred times sweeter than sugar, so a little goes a long way. It can have a bitter aftertaste if used in large quantities, so it's sometimes combined with other sweeteners to take the edge off.

- **Erythritol.** This low-calorie sweetener is found naturally in some fruits and vegetables. It's often sold under the brand name Swerve. It has very few calories and won't raise your blood sugar. Its main component doesn't get fully absorbed by the body, passing through the urine unchanged. The long-term effects of this aren't known, but no negative effects have been observed. It's a popular sweetener for keto baking and other keto cooking.

- **Monk Fruit Powder.** Extracted from a fruit that was first cultivated in China and Thailand, this sweetener has a pleasant flavor profile, and it doesn't raise blood sugar or insulin levels. It can be expensive, so it's often mixed with other sweeteners or ingredients; keto dieters should be on the lookout for this and avoid any monk fruit blends that contain other, less keto-friendly sweeteners.

SWEETENERS TO AVOID

Sugar, of course, spikes your blood sugar and insulin and can take you out of ketosis. Other sweeteners that contain carbs (e.g., agave, honey, molasses, date syrup, maple syrup, and coconut palm sugar) are often marketed as "healthier" alternatives, but on a keto diet they're just as important to skip. Sugar is sugar, whether it's white and powdery and refined in a factory or brown and sticky and distilled from tree sap. Look to the low-carb sweeteners above instead.

And look out: not all low-carb sweeteners are keto-friendly! Aspartame, saccharine, acesulfame K, and sucralose all affect insulin levels—not as much as sugar does, but still significantly. If you want to stay in ketosis, steer clear of those options.

TOP KETO TIPS

- Enlist the help of your doctor or nutritionist to decide whether keto is a healthy fit for you. (This is especially important if you are diabetic or on any medications.)
- Start your keto diet with less than 50 grams of net carbs per day (as low as 20 grams) and gradually increase, monitoring your ketone levels using a blood keto meter.
- Eat enough protein to match your weight and activity level (0.6 to 1 gram per pound or 1.3 to 2.2 grams per kilogram of lean body mass).
- Add enough fat to boost flavor, fill the rest of your energy needs, and keep you from feeling hungry between meals.
- Use your hunger as a guide; eat when you're hungry, not when you aren't.
- Ease the "keto flu" with plenty of water and electrolyte-rich foods such as avocados, leafy greens, and nuts.

- Focus on natural foods, and get your daily carbs from berries, nuts, and non-starchy veggies, when possible, to pack in more micronutrients and feel fuller and more satisfied.
- Plan ahead so you have foods on hand that fit your diet. (Explore apps and calculators that can help you calculate your keto needs and track your progress.)
- Eat a variety of healthy keto foods and recipes.

NOTE: WEIGH AND MEASURE CAREFULLY

Because the ratio of carbs to fats to proteins is so important to keto success, make sure you stick to the quantities listed in these recipes. Although most of the ingredients are given in cups, if you have a scale and can weigh your ingredients to match the given weights in grams, your creations will match the keto macros in the recipe a bit more precisely. Weigh ingredients (rather than measuring with a measuring cup) when possible to make sure that your meal ends up with the nutrient ratio you expect, and to make sure your food is as delicious as you expect.

FAVORITE KETO-FRIENDLY FOODS

As you explore keto eating and try these keto-friendly air fryer recipes, you'll find it's handy to have certain foods perpetually on your grocery list. This is by no means an exhaustive list of everything that can fit in a keto diet. It's a list of common favorites—including many of the ingredients you'll need for the recipes in this book.

MEATS, FISH, AND OTHER HIGH-PROTEIN FOODS

- bacon
- chicken
- chicken skin
- eggs
- flank steak
- ground beef
- ground chicken
- ground pork
- pork belly
- pork rinds
- pork tenderloin
- salmon
- sardines
- scallops
- shrimp
- sirloin steak

LOW-NET-CARB FRUITS

- avocado
- blackberries
- blueberries
- olives
- raspberries
- strawberries

LOW-NET-CARB VEGETABLES

- asparagus
- basil
- bell peppers
- broccoli
- Brussels sprouts
- cabbage
- carrots
- cauliflower
- cucumber
- eggplant
- green beans
- jalapeños
- jicama
- kabocha squash
- kale
- lemons
- lettuce
- limes
- mint
- mushrooms
- radishes
- spaghetti squash
- spinach
- tomatoes
- zucchini

DAIRY PRODUCTS

- cheddar cheese
- feta cheese
- full-fat cream cheese
- mozzarella cheese
- paneer
- Parmesan cheese
- sour cream
- yogurt

OILS AND FATS

- avocado oil
- butter
- coconut oil
- ghee
- olive oil
- sesame oil

SAUCES AND CONDIMENTS

- balsamic vinegar
- coconut aminos
- coconut milk
- curry paste
- ginger paste
- gochujang
- horseradish
- mayonnaise
- nut butters
- red wine vinegar
- sugar-free chocolate chips
- sugar-free ketchup
- tamari
- unsweetened fish sauce

NUTS AND SEEDS

- almonds
- Brazil nuts
- cashews
- coconut
- flaxseed meal
- hazelnuts
- hemp hearts
- macadamia nuts
- peanuts
- pecans
- psyllium husk powder
- sesame seeds
- sunflower seeds
- walnuts

FLOURS AND FLOUR SUBSTITUTES

- almond flour
- coconut flour
- pork panko

AIR FRYER BASICS

Air fryers are revolutionizing the way people cook at home. What would normally take a whole day of cooking and even more time in clean up can now be managed on a weeknight with this fantastic appliance. The way you cook and experience food is about to drastically change. Air frying food gives all the delicious crisp and crunch to your favorite fried foods without all of the excess oil used for frying. It is a sure way to spice up any kitchen.

KITCHEN TOOLS

Here are some additional things that will help you make the most out of your air fryer.

- **Parchment Cake Rounds.** Lining the basket with precut parchment rounds will save time on prep and clean up.
- **Silicone Muffin Liners.** Excellent for baking in your air fryer or for pre-portioning out your meals.
- **Thermometer.** When coating meat in crispy toppings, it is especially helpful to know what the internal temperature of the meat is without having to cut individual pieces open.
- **Mandolin.** This is a great tool for thinly slicing vegetables. It's especially helpful if you want to start air frying your own vegetable chips!
- **Microplane.** A microplane is great for grating fresh Parmesan on top of your favorite cheesy dishes or for zesting a lemon to add an extra pop of flavor.
- **Ramekins and Small Pyrex Dishes.** Specific sizes of these will depend on the size of air fryer you have. If your air fryer is small, 6- to 7-inch (15 to 18 cm) dishes should work best.
- **Skewers.** Bamboo or metal skewers work for the air fryer recipes. Bamboo skewers are used in the recipes here. Be careful if you use metal skewers because they may be hot to the touch when you remove them from the air fryer.

PANTRY STAPLES

- **Panko.** Regular panko contains wheat and is high carb and not keto-friendly. Pork panko or almond flour is the crumb coating of choice.
- **Parmesan.** Incorporating Parmesan with the above panko options can result in a dynamic combination of flavors.

- **Olive Oil Cooking Spray.** Lubricating what you're cooking before you add it to your air fryer makes cleanup as easy as cooking was.
- **Dried Spice Mix.** Sometimes all you need to add to veggies are a few simple spices to really make them pop. Some different blends you could try are taco seasoning, jerk seasoning, everything bagel seasoning, or really any pre-mixed seasoning.

ROOKIE MISTAKES

1. **Spraying the rack and not the food.** Directly spraying the rack can damage the non-stick coating.
2. **Crowding the air fryer.** Give space around it for the air to escape while cooking.
3. **Delaying cleanup.** If food residue is left to cool, it will stick and be *much* harder to clean up afterwards.
4. **Assuming that temperatures correlate to oven cooks.** It's an entirely different appliance. It's better to err on the side of caution than to burn your dinner.
5. **Thinking "Bigger is better!"** Buy the right size for your home. Air fryers can be quite bulky, and there is no need to take up more counter space than is necessary.
6. **Set it and forget it.** Rotating food isn't always necessary, but you will want to flip larger items for the final few minutes of cooking to ensure everything is crisp and cooked on all sides.

*ALL RECIPES WERE TESTED ON A CUISINART AIR FRYER. DIFFERENT MODELS OR STYLES OF AIR FRYERS MAY REQUIRE ALTERED COOKING TIMES.

BREAKFAST

BREAKFAST BISCUITS 16

GRANOLA 17

BACON EGG LOAF 18

SHEETPAN PANCAKES 20

DENVER OMELET EGG LOAF 21

FRENCH TOAST EGG LOAF 22

BREAKFAST BISCUITS

YIELD: 6 BISCUITS

PREP TIME: 15 MINUTES

COOK TIME: 13 TO

15 MINUTES

INGREDIENTS

1 tablespoon (15 ml) avocado oil

¼ cup (40 g) diced white onion

1 jalapeño, minced

½ cup (80 g) sausage crumbles, raw or precooked

1 cup (30 g) crushed pork rinds

1 teaspoon (5 g) baking powder

½ teaspoon garlic powder

½ teaspoon salt

3 large eggs

1 cup (120 g) shredded cheddar cheese

NUTRITION: 1 SERVING = 1 BISCUIT

CALORIES 247.3 KCAL

CARBOHYDRATE 2.3 G

TOTAL FAT 19.8 G

SATURATED FAT 8.4 G

TRANS FATS 0 G

SODIUM 760.5 MG

TOTAL SUGARS 0.4 G

PROTEIN 15.6 G

FIBER 0.2 G

INSTRUCTIONS

1. Heat the avocado oil in a sauté pan over medium heat. Add the onion and jalapeño. If using raw sausage, add that as well. Cook until the onions are translucent and the sausage is cooked and lightly browned on the outside, 4 to 6 minutes.

2. In a medium-size bowl, combine the crushed pork rinds, baking powder, garlic powder, and salt. Whisk to combine.

3. In a separate bowl, beat the eggs. Add the cheese and dry ingredient mixture.

4. Add the cooked sausage, onion, and jalapeño mixture. If your sausage crumbles were precooked, add them now. Stir to combine with the egg mixture.

5. Line the bottom of the air fryer tray with parchment paper or greased foil.

6. Divide the batter into 6 equal biscuits on the tray. Leave about 1 inch (2.5 cm) of space between each biscuit so the biscuits can spread. They should generally hold their shape.

7. Air-fry at 325°F (163°C) for 8 to 10 minutes, until they're crisp on top. Remove from the air fryer and allow to cool and set for 5 minutes.

8. Serve by itself as a biscuit or muffin or dip into a runny egg.

GRANOLA

YIELD: 18 SERVINGS
(1 OUNCE [28 G] EACH)
PREP TIME: 10 MINUTES
COOK TIME: 15 TO
20 MINUTES

INGREDIENTS

1 cup (145 g) raw, unsalted almonds

1 cup (120 g) raw, unsalted pecans

⅔ cup (60 g) unsweetened finely shredded coconut

½ cup (80 g) pumpkin seeds

⅓ cup (37 g) golden flaxseed meal

⅓ cup (48 g) sunflower seeds or hemp hearts

⅓ cup (75 g) unsalted butter, coconut oil, or ghee

⅓ cup (65 g) granulated sweetener (I prefer erythritol)

2 egg whites

1½ teaspoons (7 ml) vanilla extract

1 teaspoon (3 g) ground cinnamon

½ teaspoon salt, or to taste

NUTRITION: 1 SERVING = 1 OUNCE (28 G) EACH
CALORIES 203.8 KCAL
CARBOHYDRATE 2.2 G
TOTAL FAT 19 G
SATURATED FAT 5.2 G
TRANS FATS 0.1 G
SODIUM 75.4 MG
TOTAL SUGARS 1 G
PROTEIN 5.3 G
FIBER 3.7 G

INSTRUCTIONS

1. Coarsely chop the almonds and pecans and place them in a medium-size bowl. Add the coconut, pumpkin seeds, flaxseed meal, and sunflower seeds and stir to combine.

2. Melt the butter in a glass dish in the microwave for 30 to 60 seconds. Add the sweetener, egg whites, vanilla, cinnamon, and salt and stir to combine.

3. Pour the butter mixture on top of the nut mixture and stir to combine.

4. Line the air fryer tray with enough parchment paper so that it comes up over the sides. This will help later when you're trying to remove the granola. Grease the parchment paper with oil.

5. Spread the mixture in a ½-inch (1.3 cm) layer on the parchment paper and press to compact.

6. Air-fry at 250°F (120°C) for 15 to 20 minutes, or until crispy on top.

7. Remove the granola from the air fryer with the parchment paper and allow to completely cool on a drying rack. It will harden as it cools.

8. Break apart the granola once it is cooled and store it in the fridge in an airtight container.

BACON EGG LOAF

YIELD: 4 MINI LOAVES
PREP TIME: 10 MINUTES
COOK TIME: 12 TO
15 MINUTES

INGREDIENTS

4 large eggs

½ cup (120 g) cream cheese, softened

2 tablespoons (28 g) unsalted butter, melted

¼ cup (7.5 g) crushed pork rinds or (28 g) almond flour

2 tablespoons (10 g) bacon crumbles

½ teaspoon salt

Mini silicone loaf cups
  5.8 x 2.8 x 1.2 inches
  (14.5 x 7.1 x 3 cm)

INSTRUCTIONS

1. Place the eggs, cream cheese, melted butter, crushed pork rinds, bacon crumbles, and salt in a bowl. You can mix the loaf ingredients in a food processor, with a stand mixer, or by hand. Mixing with a food processor will make the egg loaf light and aerated and pulverize the bacon crumbles.

2. Grease 4 mini silicone loaf cups. Carefully pour the egg mixture into the mini loaf cups so that they're three-fourths full with the mixture.

3. Air-fry on the lower rack at 300°F (150°C) for 12 to 15 minutes. They're done when a toothpick inserted in the bottom of the loaf and comes out clean. The tops might get a little bit brown.

4. Allow loaves to cool for 5 minutes on a drying rack and serve warm or cold (like a quiche).

NUTRITION: 1 SERVING = 1 LOAF (¼ RECIPE)
CALORIES 288.4 KCAL
CARBOHYDRATE 2.1 G
TOTAL FAT 27.7 G
SATURATED FAT 12.2 G
TRANS FATS 0.6 G
SODIUM 356.7 MG
TOTAL SUGARS 0 G
PROTEIN 14.6 G
FIBER 0.3 G

TIP: SILICONE MUFFIN LINERS WILL WORK, TOO, IF YOU ARE UNABLE TO FIND THE LOAF STYLE.

SHEETPAN PANCAKES

YIELD: 10 PANCAKES
PREP TIME: 20 MINUTES
COOK TIME: 20 MINUTES

INGREDIENTS

2 cups (224 g) almond flour

⅓ cup (65 g) granulated sweetener (I prefer erythritol)

3 tablespoons (24 g) coconut flour

2 teaspoons (10 g) baking powder

1 teaspoon (5 g) psyllium husk powder

¼ cup (56 g) cream cheese, softened

8 large eggs

2 tablespoons (30 ml) vanilla extract

TIP: USE THE CONVECTION/BAKE SETTING IF YOUR AIR FRYER HAS IT. THIS WILL COOK THE BOTTOM MORE THOROUGHLY.

NUTRITION: 1 SERVING = 2.5 PANCAKES (1/4 RECIPE)
CALORIES 217.7 KCAL
CARBOHYDRATE 6.7 G
TOTAL FAT 17.5 G
SATURATED FAT 3.5 G
TRANS FATS 0.1 G
SODIUM 178.3 MG
TOTAL SUGARS 1.5 G
PROTEIN 10.1 G
FIBER 3.6 G

INSTRUCTIONS

1. Place the almond flour, sweetener, coconut flour, baking powder, and psyllium husk powder in a medium-size bowl and whisk to combine.

2. In a separate large bowl, using a hand mixer or blender, mix the eggs, cream cheese, and vanilla until there are no clumps of cream cheese.

3. Add the dry mixture and blend to thoroughly combine. Allow it to rest for 15 minutes.

4. Line the air fryer tray with enough parchment paper so that it comes up over the sides. This will help later when you're trying to remove the pancakes. Grease the parchment paper with oil.

5. Pour batter onto the parchment paper. It should not go over two-thirds the height of the tray.

6. Air-fry at 250°F (120°C) for 20 minutes, or until a toothpick inserted into the center comes out clean and the top is golden brown.

7. Remove the pancake from the air fryer and allow it to rest for 5 minutes. Pull up on the parchment to lift the pancake out of the tray. Cut it into 10 equal pieces.

8. The pancakes can be served with pancake toppings if they are eaten fresh. I store them in the fridge for on-the-go eating. Store them in the fridge for up to a week for an easy weekday breakfast.

DENVER OMELET EGG LOAF

YIELD: 4 MINI LOAVES
PREP TIME: 10 MINUTES
COOK TIME: 17 TO
20 MINUTES

INGREDIENTS

1 tablespoon (15 ml) avocado oil

2 tablespoons (20 g) diced
   yellow onion

¼ cup (37 g) diced bell pepper
   (any color you like)

4 large eggs

½ cup (120 g) cream cheese, softened

2 tablespoons (28 g) unsalted
   butter, melted

¼ cup (7.5 g) crushed pork rinds or
   (28 g) almond flour

¼ cup (30 g) shredded cheddar cheese

¼ cup (37.5 g) diced ham

½ teaspoon salt

Mini silicone loaf cups
   5.8 x 2.8 x 1.2 inches
   (14.5 x 7.1 x 3 cm)

NUTRITION: 1 SERVING = 1 LOAF (1/4 RECIPE)
CALORIES 318.9 KCAL
CARBOHYDRATE 3.2 G
TOTAL FAT 28.2 G
SATURATED FAT 13.4 G
TRANS FATS 0.6 G
SODIUM 630.4 MG
TOTAL SUGARS 1.8 G
PROTEIN 14.1 G
FIBER 0.3 G

INSTRUCTIONS

1. Heat the avocado oil in a cast-iron skillet over medium heat.

2. Add the diced onion and bell pepper to the skillet and cook until translucent, 4 to 6 minutes.

3. Transfer the cooked onion and pepper to a bowl and add eggs, cream cheese, butter, pork rinds, cheese, ham, and salt. You can mix the loaf ingredients in a food processor, with a stand mixer, or by hand. Mixing with a food processor will make the omelet light and aerated and the ingredients will be small pieces.

4. Grease 4 mini silicone loaf cups. Fill the cups two-thirds full with the mixture. The number you need will depend on their size.

5. Air-fry on the lower rack at 300°F (150°C) for 12 to 15 minutes. They're done when a toothpick inserted in the bottom of the loaf and comes out clean. The tops might get a little bit brown.

6. Allow loaves to cool for 5 minutes on a drying rack and serve warm or cold (like a quiche).

TIP: SILICONE MUFFIN LINERS WILL WORK, TOO, IF YOU ARE UNABLE TO FIND THE LOAF STYLE.

FRENCH TOAST EGG LOAF

YIELD: 4 MINI LOAVES
PREP TIME: 10 MINUTES
COOK TIME: 12 TO
15 MINUTES

INGREDIENTS

4 large eggs

½ cup (120 g) cream cheese, softened

2 tablespoons (28 g) unsalted butter, melted

¼ cup (7.5 g) crushed pork rinds or (28 g) almond flour

3 tablespoons (36 g) granulated sugar substitute (e.g., Swerve)

1 teaspoon (5 ml) vanilla extract

1 teaspoon (3 g) ground cinnamon

½ teaspoon salt

Mini silicone loaf cups
5.8 x 2.8 x 1.2 inches
(14.5 x 7.1 x 3 cm)

INSTRUCTIONS

1. Place the eggs, cream cheese, butter, pork rinds, sugar substitute, vanilla, cinnamon, and salt in a bowl. You can mix the loaf ingredients in a food processor, with a stand mixer, or by hand. Mixing with a food processor will make a smoother French toast loaf.

2. Grease 4 individual mini silicone loaf cups. Fill the cups two-thirds full with the mixture.

3. Air-fry on the lower rack at 300°F (150°C) for 12 to 15 minutes. The loaves are done when a toothpick inserted in the bottom of the loaf and comes out clean. The tops might get a little bit brown.

4. Allow loaves to cool for 5 minutes on a drying rack and serve warm or cold (like a quiche).

NUTRITION: 1 SERVING = 1 LOAF (¼ RECIPE)
CALORIES 254.9 KCAL
CARBOHYDRATE 2.2 G
TOTAL FAT 22.4 G
SATURATED FAT 11.4 G
TRANS FATS 0.6 G
SODIUM 526.2 MG
TOTAL SUGARS 3.7 G
PROTEIN 11.2 G
FIBER 0.3 G

SIDE DISHES

7.2 G NET CARBS = 24.2 G CARBOHYDRATES - 17 G FIBER

AVOCADO FRIES

YIELD: 16 AVOCADO FRIES
PREP TIME: 15 MINUTES
COOK TIME: 8 MINUTES

INGREDIENTS

2 underripe avocados

1 egg

½ cup (54 g) Crumb Coating (page 152)

½ teaspoon salt

¼ cup (38 g) Everything Sauce (optional, page 138)

INSTRUCTIONS

1. Cut the avocados in half lengthwise. Remove the pits and peel.

2. Cut each avocado half into quarters lengthwise, making approximately 1-inch (2.5 cm) thick "fries."

3. Grease the air fryer basket (or use greased foil or parchment paper if your air fryer cautions against greasing the rack).

4. Beat the egg in a medium-size shallow baking dish and add a splash of water.

5. Place the crumb coating into a second shallow dish.

6. Dip each avocado fry into the egg wash and then into the crumb coating, covering it completely.

7. Air-fry at 400°F (200°C) for 4 minutes per side, or until crispy.

8. Remove the avocado fries from the air fryer basket with a spatula or tongs and sprinkle with the salt.

9. Serve with the sauce, if desired.

NUTRITION: 1 SERVING = 8 FRIES
CALORIES 431.9 KCAL
CARBOHYDRATE 24.2 G
TOTAL FAT 35.2 G
SATURATED FAT 7.6 G
TRANS FATS 0 G
SODIUM 734.4 MG
TOTAL SUGARS 7.4 G
PROTEIN 25.8 G
FIBER 17 G

1.8 G NET CARBS = 2.2 G CARBOHYDRATES - 0.4 G FIBER

BACON JALAPEÑO POPPERS

YIELD: 24 POPPERS,
6 SERVINGS
PREP TIME: 15 TO
20 MINUTES
COOK TIME: 12 MINUTES

INGREDIENTS

8 ounces (224 g) cream cheese, softened

½ cup (120 ml) pickle juice

1 teaspoon (3 g) garlic powder

12 jalapeños

¼ cup (28 g) crumbled bacon

INSTRUCTIONS

1. Combine cream cheese, pickle juice, and garlic powder in a medium-size bowl or the bowl of a stand mixer with a paddle attachment and mix until it is a thin frosting consistency. Spoon the mixture into a piping bag or plastic bag and refrigerate while you prep the jalapeños.

2. Slice the jalapeños lengthwise with a paring knife. Remove and discard the ribs and seeds.

3. Place the jalapeños in the air fryer basket and air-fry at 350°F (180°C) for 8 minutes.

4. Carefully remove the jalapeños from the air fryer and add the bacon crumbles to the centers.

5. Remove the cream cheese mixture from the fridge and pipe it over the bacon crumbles.

6. Air-fry the jalapeños at 400°F (200°C) for 4 minutes, or until the cheese on top is golden brown.

7. The jalapeños will be a bit tender, so handle with care with either tongs or a spatula.

NUTRITION: 1 SERVING
= 4 POPPERS
CALORIES 81.2 KCAL
CARBOHYDRATE 2.2 G
TOTAL FAT 7.2 G
SATURATED FAT 4.2 G
TRANS FATS 0.2 G
SODIUM 101.6 MG
TOTAL SUGARS 1.2 G
PROTEIN 2 G
FIBER 0.4 G

CHICKEN SKIN CHIPS

YIELD: **4 SERVINGS**
CHICKEN SKIN CHIPS
PREP TIME: **5 MINUTES**
COOK TIME: **8 MINUTES**

INGREDIENTS

1 pound (454 g) chicken skin
2 teaspoons (12 g) salt

INSTRUCTIONS

1. Lay out the chicken skin on a clean surface and pat dry with paper towels.

2. Sprinkle the salt on the chicken skins generously and then flip to salt the other side.

3. Place parchment paper in the air fryer basket and grease with oil.

4. Place the chicken skins on the parchment. They should not be touching or layered.

5. Air-fry (in batches, if needed) at 375°F (190°C) for 4 minutes per side, until crispy. Watch carefully to make sure the chicken skins do not burn.

6. Allow the chips to cool on a wire rack. They will keep in an air-tight container in the fridge for 5 to 7 days.

NUTRITION: 1 SERVING = ¼ RECIPE
CALORIES 514.8 KCAL
CARBOHYDRATE 0 G
TOTAL FAT 46.1 G
SATURATED FAT 13 G
TRANS FATS 1 G
SODIUM 1252.6 MG
TOTAL SUGARS 0 G
PROTEIN 23.1 G
FIBER 0 G

COCONUT-CRUSTED PANEER

YIELD: 8 SERVINGS
PREP TIME: 15 MINUTES
COOK TIME: 6 MINUTES

INGREDIENTS

1 pound (454 g) paneer cheese

1 teaspoon (6 g) salt

¾ teaspoon garam masala

¼ teaspoon curry powder

¼ teaspoon ground ginger

¼ teaspoon smoked paprika

1 tablespoon (8 g) coconut flour

1 large egg

½ cup (40 g) coconut flakes

½ cup (15 g) ground pork rinds

INSTRUCTIONS

1. Slice the paneer into 1-inch (2.5 cm) cubes.

2. Place parchment paper on the air fryer rack and grease with oil.

3. In a medium-size bowl, combine the salt, garam marsala, curry powder, ground ginger, paprika, and coconut flour. Whisk and set aside.

4. In a second medium-size bowl, beat the egg with a splash of water to make an egg wash.

5. In another medium-size bowl, stir the coconut flakes and crushed pork rinds to combine and set aside.

6. One by one, dip the paneer cubes into the spice mixture and roll around to coat. Then dip the cube in the egg wash. Finally, coat the cube with the coconut/pork rind mixture to fully cover.

7. Place the cubes in your air fryer, trying to keep them in a single layer with about ¼ inch (6 mm) of space between them. Air-fry them at 375°F (190°C) for 6 minutes. They should be golden brown and will *not* be gooey on the inside.

8. Remove the paneer with a spatula and serve immediately as a finger food or with toothpicks.

NUTRITION: 1 SERVING = 1/8 RECIPE
CALORIES 266.8 KCAL
CARBOHYDRATE 2.9 G
TOTAL FAT 22 G
SATURATED FAT 14.3 G
TRANS FATS 0.4 G
SODIUM 407.8 MG
TOTAL SUGARS 1.6 G
PROTEIN 15 G
FIBER 1.2 G

COCONUT CURRY PANEER

YIELD: 6 SERVINGS
PREP TIME: 5 MINUTES
COOK TIME: 6 MINUTES

INGREDIENTS

1 pound (454 g) paneer

1 tablespoon (15 ml) avocado oil

1 teaspoon (6 g) salt

¾ teaspoon garam masala

¼ teaspoon curry powder

¼ teaspoon ground ginger

¼ teaspoon smoked paprika

1 recipe Coconut Curry Peanut Sauce (page 135)

INSTRUCTIONS

1. Slice the paneer into 1-inch (2.5 cm) cubes. Place the cubes in a large bowl.

2. Add the avocado oil, salt, garam masala, curry powder, ground ginger, and paprika. Toss to coat.

3. Add the paneer to your air fryer, trying to keep the cubes in a single layer with about ¼ inch (6 mm) of space between them. Air-fry at 375°F (190°C) for 6 minutes. The cubes should be golden brown and will *not* be gooey on the inside.

4. Transfer the paneer to a bowl, add the sauce, and toss to coat. Eat as is or serve over cauliflower rice.

NUTRITION: 1 SERVING
CALORIES 327.7 KCAL
CARBOHYDRATE 3.5 G
TOTAL FAT 28.6 G
SATURATED FAT 17.7 G
TRANS FATS 0.4 G
SODIUM 313 MG
TOTAL SUGARS 2.3 G
PROTEIN 13.5 G
FIBER 0.6 G

2.5 G NET CARBS = 4.4 G CARBOHYDRATES - 1.9 G FIBER

JALAPEÑO-STUFFED MUSHROOMS

YIELD: 4 SERVINGS
PREP TIME: 15 MINUTES
COOK TIME: 13 MINUTES

INGREDIENTS

2 small-medium jalapeños

1 pound (454 g) whole button mushroom

½ cup (120 g) cream cheese, softened

¼ cup (60 ml) pickle juice

½ teaspoon garlic powder

3 tablespoons (15 g) bacon crumbles

Salt to taste

NUTRITION: 1 SERVING = ¼ RECIPE
CALORIES 153 KCAL
CARBOHYDRATE 4.4 G
TOTAL FAT 11.6 G
SATURATED FAT 6.5 G
TRANS FATS 0.3 G
SODIUM 192.3 MG
TOTAL SUGARS 1.7 G
PROTEIN 7.1 G
FIBER 1.9 G

INSTRUCTIONS

1. Slice the jalapeños lengthwise with a paring knife. Remove and discard the ribs and seeds. Remove the stems from the mushroom caps, reserving the stems, and wipe off any excess dirt from the mushrooms.

2. Air-fry the jalapeños and mushroom stems at 400°F (200°C) for 8 minutes.

3. While the jalapeños are cooking, combine the cream cheese, pickle juice, and garlic powder in a medium-size bowl or the bowl of a stand mixer with a paddle attachment and mix until it is a thin frosting consistency.

4. Allow the cooked jalapeños and mushroom stems to cool slightly, then dice. Add both to the cream cheese mixture and fold in to incorporate.

5. Spray the tops of the mushrooms caps with the avocado oil spray and sprinkle them with a pinch of salt.

6. Use a spoon to fill the mushroom caps with the cream cheese mixture. Try to get it into the crevices inside the edges of the mushroom caps.

7. Place the mushrooms, cream cheese facing up, in the air fryer basket. It's okay if they're touching. Air-fry at 400°F (200°C) for 5 minutes, or until the cream cheese is golden brown.

8. Remove carefully and serve immediately.

JICAMA FRIES

YIELD: 2 SERVINGS
PREP TIME: 10 MINUTES
COOK TIME: 30 TO
35 MINUTES

INGREDIENTS

1 medium jicama (or precut sticks from the produce section)

2 tablespoons (10 g) grated Parmesan

½ teaspoon garlic powder

½ teaspoon paprika

½ teaspoon salt

2 tablespoons (30 ml) avocado oil

¼ cup (38 g) Everything Sauce (page 138) or sugar-free ketchup (optional)

INSTRUCTIONS

1. Bring a medium-sized pot of salted water to a boil over high heat.

2. Peel and slice the jicama into ¼-inch (6 mm) wide sticks.

3. Boil the jicama fries for about 10 minutes, until they are al dente in texture.

4. Drain the sticks and pat them dry with a paper towel or clean dish towel.

5. In a medium-size bowl, stir the Parmesan, garlic powder, paprika, and salt to combine.

6. In another bowl, toss the jicama sticks with the avocado oil. Then toss them with the seasoning mixture.

7. Spread the fires on the air fryer rack in a single layer.

8. Air-fry the fries at 350°F (180°C) for 20 to 25 minutes, checking often to make sure they aren't burning.

9. Serve with the sauce, if desired.

NUTRITION: 1 SERVING = ½ RECIPE
CALORIES 276.2 KCAL
CARBOHYDRATE 30.8 G
TOTAL FAT 15.7 G
SATURATED FAT 2.6 G
TRANS FATS 0.1 G
SODIUM 716.3 MG
TOTAL SUGARS 6 G
PROTEIN 4.4 G
FIBER 16.4 G

PARMESAN-CRUSTED ZUCCHINI SPEARS

YIELD: 8 ZUCCHINI SPEARS

PREP TIME: 10 MINUTES

COOK TIME: 7 TO 10 MINUTES

INGREDIENTS

2 zucchinis

1 large egg

½ cup (50 g) grated Parmesan

½ teaspoon salt

INSTRUCTIONS

1. Cut the zucchinis in half lengthwise. Then cut those halves lengthwise again to make 4 spears per zucchini. They should end up less than 1 inch (2.5 cm) across, and if they're not, cut them down to size.

2. Beat the egg in a medium-size shallow baking dish and add a splash of water to create an egg wash.

3. Place the grated Parmesan in a second shallow dish.

4. Dip the flesh side of the zucchini in the egg wash and then into the grated Parmesan, pressing down to adhere the Parmesan to the egg wash. Sprinkle with a pinch of salt.

5. Place parchment paper or foil in the basket of the air fryer and place the zucchini fries on top. They can be close, but not pressed together. Try not to stack them.

6. Air-fry the spears at 400°F (200°C) for 7 to 10 minutes, or until golden brown. Remove them carefully with a spatula and serve immediately.

NUTRITION: 1 SERVING = 4 ZUCCHINI SPEARS

CALORIES 173.2 KCAL

CARBOHYDRATE 9.6 G

TOTAL FAT 9 G

SATURATED FAT 4.8 G

TRANS FATS 0.4 G

SODIUM 1091.2MG

TOTAL SUGARS 4.8 G

PROTEIN 12.4 G

FIBER 2 G

MOZZARELLA STICKS

YIELD: 8 MOZZARELLA
STICKS
PREP TIME: 15 MINUTES +
2 HOURS IN THE FREEZER
COOK TIME: 6 TO
8 MINUTES

INGREDIENTS

4 full-fat mozzarella sticks
1 large egg
1 serving Crumb Coating
   (page 152)
2 tablespoons (7.2 g)
   Italian seasoning
½ cup (120 ml) sugar-free marinara
   sauce (e.g., Rao's)

TIP: YOU CAN PREP THE CRUMBED
MOZZARELLA STICKS THE DAY BEFORE AND
LEAVE THEM IN THE FREEZER UNTIL YOU'RE
READY TO SERVE.

NUTRITION: 1 SERVING = 4 MOZZARELLA STICKS
CALORIES 306 KCAL
CARBOHYDRATE 1.2 G
TOTAL FAT 21.6 G
SATURATED FAT 10.4 G
TRANS FATS 0 G
SODIUM 716 MG
TOTAL SUGARS 0.4 G
PROTEIN 28 G
FIBER 0 G

INSTRUCTIONS

1. Line a baking sheet with parchment paper. Cut the mozzarella sticks in half, place them on the prepared baking sheet, and freeze for them at least 1 hour.

2. When ready, beat the egg in a medium-size shallow baking dish and add a splash of water to create an egg wash.

3. In a second shallow dish, stir the crumb coating and seasoning to combine.

4. Remove the mozzarella sticks from the freezer and dip each in the egg wash and then in the crumb coating. Press and flip the sticks in the crumb mixture to coat thoroughly.

5. Return the mozzarella sticks to the parchment-lined baking sheet and freeze them for another hour at least.

6. Grease the air fryer basket (if your air fryer warns against this, use foil and flip the mozzarella sticks halfway through for maximum crispiness).

7. Air-fry the mozzarella sticks at 400°F (200°C) for 6 to 8 minutes, or until the coating is golden brown.

8. Serve the mozzarella sticks with the marinara sauce.

23.7 G NET CARBS = 28.2 G CARBOHYDRATES - 4.5 G FIBER

ROASTED RADISHES

YIELD: **4 SERVINGS**
PREP TIME: **6 MINUTES**
COOK TIME: **10 MINUTES**

INGREDIENTS

2 cups (360 g) halved red radishes

1 tablespoon (14 g) unsalted butter, melted

1 teaspoon (6 g) salt

½ teaspoon garlic powder

½ teaspoon dried thyme

INSTRUCTIONS

1. In a medium-size bowl, combine the radishes, melted butter, salt, garlic powder, and thyme and toss gently to coat the radishes.

2. Line the air fryer basket with aluminum foil and add the radishes. Air-fry the radishes at 350°F (180°C) for 10 minutes, or until lightly browned and crispy.

3. Enjoy the radishes immediately.

NUTRITION: 1 SERVING = ¼ RECIPE
CALORIES 27.1 KCAL
CARBOHYDRATE 28.2 G
TOTAL FAT 2.9 G
SATURATED FAT 1.8 G
TRANS FATS 0.1 G
SODIUM 623.5 MG
TOTAL SUGARS 23.4 G
PROTEIN 1.2 G
FIBER 4.5 G

PICKLE FRIES

YIELD: 16 PICKLE FRIES
PREP TIME: 10 MINUTES
COOK TIME: 6 MINUTES

INGREDIENTS

4 large whole pickles

1 large egg

¼ cup (27 g) Crumb Coating
(page 152)

INSTRUCTIONS

1. Remove the pickles from the brine and shake gently to remove any excess moisture. Cut the pickles lengthwise into quarters, making 1-inch (2.5 cm) thick "fries."

2. Beat the egg in a medium-size shallow baking dish and add a splash of water to create an egg wash.

3. Place the crumb coating in a second shallow dish.

4. Dip the seed-side of each pickle fry in the egg wash and then in the crumb coating. Press them in the crumb mixture to coat thoroughly.

5. Place parchment paper in the bottom of the basket and grease with oil. Place the fries in the basket, crumb-side up.

6. Air-fry the pickles at 400°F (200°C) for 6 minutes, or until the breading is crispy.

7. Carefully remove the fries (they may be floppy if the pickles were not firm) and serve immediately.

NUTRITION: 1 SERVING = 8 FRIES
CALORIES 120.8 KCAL
CARBOHYDRATE 7.2 G
TOTAL FAT 6.4 G
SATURATED FAT 5.2 G
TRANS FATS 1.2 G
SODIUM 2370.4 MG
TOTAL SUGARS 3.2 G
PROTEIN 9.6 G
FIBER 2.4 G

4.2 G NET CARBS = 5.4 G CARBOHYDRATES - 1.2 G FIBER

JALAPEÑO ZUCCHINI BOATS

YIELD: **4 ZUCCHINI BOATS**
PREP TIME: **15 MINUTES**
COOK TIME: **17 TO 19 MINUTES**

INGREDIENTS

2 small-medium jalapeños

2 zucchinis

Avocado oil cooking spray

Salt, to taste

½ cup (120 g) cream cheese, softened

¼ cup (60 ml) pickle juice

½ teaspoon garlic powder

¼ cup (20 g) bacon crumbles

TIP: TRY REPLACING THE BACON CRUMBLES WITH PRECOOKED PULLED PORK.

NUTRITION: 1 SERVING = 1 BOAT
CALORIES 180 KCAL
CARBOHYDRATE 5.4 G
TOTAL FAT 14.2 G
SATURATED FAT 7.8 G
TRANS FATS 0.3 G
SODIUM 350.4 MG
TOTAL SUGARS 3.8 G
PROTEIN 7.1 G
FIBER 1.2 G

INSTRUCTIONS

1. Slice the jalapeños lengthwise with a paring knife. Remove and discard the ribs and seeds.

2. Cut the zucchini lengthwise and scrape out the seeds to hollow it out into a boat. Spray it with avocado oil and top with a pinch of salt.

3. Air-fry the jalapeños and zucchini boats at 375°F (190°C) for 8 minutes.

4. Meanwhile, mix the cream cheese, pickle juice, and garlic powder in a medium-size bowl or the bowl of a stand mixer with a paddle attachment until it is a thin frosting consistency.

5. Remove the jalapeños from the air fryer but leave the zucchini for another 4 minutes.

6. Dice the jalapeño, add it to the cream cheese mixture, and stir to incorporate.

7. Carefully remove the boats from the air fryer and fill them with a layer of crumbled bacon.

8. Divide the cream cheese mixture among the zucchini halves and spoon it into the boats.

9. Return the zucchini boats to the air fryer and air-fry at 375°F (190°C) 5 to 7 minutes, or until the cheese is golden brown. Remove them carefully and serve immediately.

PROTEIN JALAPEÑO MUFFINS

YIELD: 8 MUFFINS
PREP TIME: 10 MINUTES
COOK TIME: 20 MINUTES

INGREDIENTS

3 ounces (84 g) crushed pork rinds

3 ounces (84 g) shredded mozzarella

4 large eggs

4 tablespoons (56 g) unsalted butter, softened

2 teaspoons (6 g) garlic powder

2 teaspoons (10 g) baking powder

1 teaspoon (6 g) salt

¼ cup (60 g) roughly chopped pickled jalapeño

Silicone muffin liners

INSTRUCTIONS

1. Mix the pork rinds, mozzarella, eggs, butter, garlic powder, baking powder, and salt thoroughly in food processor.

2. Add the jalapeño and pulse lightly to incorporate but not pulverize.

3. Grease 8 silicone muffin liners and fill them three-fourths of the way full with the batter.

4. Air-fry the muffins on the lower rack at 300°F (150°C) for 20 minutes.

5. Remove the muffins from the air fryer and wait 5 minutes. Then, remove the muffins from the liners and allow them to cool. They will keep in the fridge for about a week.

TIP: USE THE CONVECTION/BAKE SETTING IF YOUR AIR FRYER HAS IT. YOU WILL END UP WITH A CRISPY BOTTOM TO THE MUFFIN.

NUTRITION: 1 SERVING = 1 MUFFIN
CALORIES 168.9 KCAL
CARBOHYDRATE 2.2 G
TOTAL FAT 12.7 G
SATURATED FAT 5.8 G
TRANS FATS 0.2 G
SODIUM 847.6 MG
TOTAL SUGARS 0.6 G
PROTEIN 12.5 G
FIBER 0.4 G

STAR INGREDIENT
BEEF

5.5 G NET CARBS = 7.4 G CARBOHYDRATES - 1.9 G FIBER

FAJITA ROLL-UPS

YIELD: 4 ROLL-UPS
PREP TIME: 15 MINUTES +
2 HOURS MARINATING
COOK TIME: 8 TO
10 MINUTES

INGREDIENTS

2 bell peppers

½ yellow onion

2 tablespoons (30 ml) lime juice

1 tablespoon (15 ml) avocado oil

2 teaspoons (12 g) salt

1 teaspoon (3 g) chili powder

1 teaspoon (3 g) garlic powder

1 pound (454 g) sirloin steak,
    thinly sliced

Salt and ground pepper, to taste

INSTRUCTIONS

1. Thinly slice the bell pepper and yellow onion. Transfer them to a large bowl. Add the lime juice, avocado oil, salt, chili powder, and garlic powder and toss to coat. For added flavor, allow the mixture to marinate for up to 2 hours.

2. Season the steak slices with salt and pepper. These will be what you use for wraps. Divide the peppers and onions evenly among the steak slices and roll them up.

3. Line the air fryer basket with foil and lay the wraps, seam-side down, on the air fryer basket. If a wrap won't stay closed, use toothpicks to secure it.

4. Air-fry the roll-ups on the lower rack at 350°F (180°C) for 8 to 10 minutes. Check for your desired level of the steak's doneness with a paring knife, and remove the roll-ups when you are satisfied. Serve immediately.

NUTRITION: 1 SERVING
CALORIES 243.2 KCAL
CARBOHYDRATE 7.4 G
TOTAL FAT 8.8 G
SATURATED FAT 2.4 G
TRANS FATS 0.2 G
SODIUM 1278 MG
TOTAL SUGARS 3.7 G
PROTEIN 35 G
FIBER 1.9 G

4.9 G NET CARBS = 6 G CARBOHYDRATES - 1.1 G FIBER

FLANK STEAK WITH CHIMICHURRI

YIELD: 4 SERVINGS
PREP TIME: 5 MINUTES +
5 MINUTES RESTING
COOK TIME: 10 TO
12 MINUTES

INGREDIENTS

1 pound (454 g) flank steak

1 teaspoon (5 ml) avocado oil

½ teaspoon salt

½ teaspoon garlic powder

Juice of 1 lime

½ cup (120 ml) Chimichurri
  (page 136)

INSTRUCTIONS

1. Rub the steak with the avocado oil, salt, and garlic powder.

2. Air-fry the steak on the top rack at 400°F (200°C) for 5 to 6 minutes per side, depending on the thickness of the steak. Check for your desired level of the steak's doneness with a paring knife, and remove it when you are satisfied. Let it rest for 5 minutes.

3. Drizzle the steak with the lime juice and cut it against the grain.

4. Serve the steak with the chimichurri.

NUTRITION: 1 SERVING = ¼ RECIPE
CALORIES 400.4 KCAL
CARBOHYDRATE 6 G
TOTAL FAT 26.8 G
SATURATED FAT 4.4 G
TRANS FATS 0.2 G
SODIUM 972.9 MG
TOTAL SUGARS 1.5 G
PROTEIN 35.1 G
FIBER 1.1 G

5.9 G NET CARBS = 6.6 G CARBOHYDRATES - 0.7 G FIBER

GREEK MEATBALLS

YIELD: 20 MEATBALLS,
4 SERVINGS
PREP TIME: 15 MINUTES
COOK TIME: 8 MINUTES

INGREDIENTS

8 ounces (227 g) lean ground beef

8 ounces (227 g) ground pork

¼ cup (7.5 g) ground pork rinds

2 ounces (56 g) feta cheese, crumbled

1 large egg, lightly beaten

¼ cup (30 g) finely chopped
   mint leaves

¼ cup (40 g) finely diced onion or
   ½ teaspoon onion powder

2 cloves garlic, minced

3 tablespoons (45 ml) lemon juice

1 teaspoon (2 g) dried oregano

1 teaspoon (2 g) ground cumin

½ teaspoon ground coriander

¼ teaspoon ground cinnamon

1 teaspoon (6 g) salt

1 cup (120 g) Tzatziki Sauce
   (page 148)

INSTRUCTIONS

1. Combine the beef, pork, pork rinds, feta, egg, mint, onion, garlic, lemon juice, oregano, cumin, coriander, cinnamon, and salt in a large bowl. With clean hands, knead the mixture to evenly distribute all the ingredients.

2. Grease a wire air fryer rack (or use greased foil or parchment paper if your air fryer cautions against greasing the rack).

3. Use a cookie scoop to make 20 meatballs and place them in your air fryer. They will cook best if they're close but not touching, so you may have to air-fry them in batches.

4. Air-fry the meatballs at 400°F (200°C) for 8 minutes. If you are using foil, flip the meatballs over halfway through the cooking time.

5. Serve the meatballs with the tzatziki sauce.

NUTRITION: 1 SERVING = 5 MEATBALLS
CALORIES 431.1 KCAL
CARBOHYDRATE 6.6 G
TOTAL FAT 27.9 G
SATURATED FAT 11.1 G
TRANS FATS 0.7 G
SODIUM 926.1 MG
TOTAL SUGARS 3.6 G
PROTEIN 37.9 G
FIBER 0.7 G

ITALIAN MEATBALLS

YIELD: 20 MEATBALLS,
4 SERVINGS
PREP TIME: 15 MINUTES
COOK TIME: 8 MINUTES

INGREDIENTS

1 pound (454 g) ground beef

1 pound (454 g) ground pork

2 large eggs

1 cup (120 g) shredded mozzarella

2 teaspoons (12 g) salt

1½ ounces (42 g) ground pork rinds

1 tablespoon (3.6 g)
   Italian seasoning

1 teaspoon (3 g) garlic powder

½ cup (120 ml) sugar-free
   marinara sauce (e.g., Rao's)

INSTRUCTIONS

1. Combine all the meatball ingredients in a large bowl. With clean hands, knead the mixture to evenly distribute all the ingredients.

2. Grease a wire air fryer rack (or use greased foil or parchment paper if your air fryer cautions against greasing the rack).

3. Use a cookie scoop to make 20 meatballs and place them in your air fryer. They will cook best if they're close but not touching, so you may have to air-fry them in batches.

4. Air-fry the meatballs at 400°F (200°C) for 8 minutes. If you are using foil, flip the meatballs over halfway through the cooking time.

5. Serve the meatballs with the marinara sauce.

NUTRITION: 1 SERVING = 5 MEATBALLS
CALORIES 472.6 KCAL
CARBOHYDRATE 2.8 G
TOTAL FAT 30.9 G
SATURATED FAT 11.7 G
TRANS FATS 0.6 G
SODIUM 1592.4 MG
TOTAL SUGARS 0.5 G
PROTEIN 45.2 G
FIBER 0.4 G

SPICY BEEF BULGOGI

YIELD: 4 SERVINGS

PREP TIME: 20 MINUTES +
1 HOUR MARINATING

COOK TIME: 6 TO
8 MINUTES

INGREDIENTS

⅓ cup (80 ml) coconut aminos

3 cloves garlic, minced

3 tablespoons (36 g) brown sugar substitute (e.g., Swerve)

2 tablespoons (30 ml) sesame oil

1 tablespoon (8 g) ginger paste

1 tablespoon (8 g) Korean Gochujang (page 142)

1 pound (454 g) shaved beef

⅛ teaspoon glucomannan

2 scallions, thinly sliced at an angle (optional)

1 teaspoon (3 g) toasted sesame seeds (optional)

TIP: YOU CAN REPLACE THE BEEF WITH PORK OR THE COCONUT AMINOS WITH TAMARI.

NUTRITION: 1 SERVING = ¼ RECIPE
CALORIES 288.8 KCAL
CARBOHYDRATE 5.4 G
TOTAL FAT 19 G
SATURATED FAT 5 G
TRANS FATS 0 G
SODIUM 464.3 MG
TOTAL SUGARS 4.3 G
PROTEIN 22.4 G
FIBER 0.2 GG

INSTRUCTIONS

1. Combine the coconut aminos, minced garlic, brown sugar substitute, sesame oil, ginger paste, and gochujang in a bowl and whisk to combine into a thin sauce.

2. Remove ¼ cup (60 ml) of the sauce and place it in a bowl or baking dish with the meat. Coat the meat evenly and let it marinate for at least 1 hour.

3. Add the glucomannan to the remaining sauce. The sauce will thicken in approximately 15 minutes.

4. Remove the meat from the marinade and air-fry it at 450°F (230°C) for 6 to 8 minutes, or until slightly crispy.

5. While the meat is cooking, heat the remaining sauce in a saucepan over low heat. Add the cooked meat to the sauce and stir to incorporate.

6. Top the meat with the scallions and sesame seeds, if desired. Serve immediately as is or with cauliflower rice.

9.7 G NET CARBS = 14.3 G CARBOHYDRATES - 4.6 G FIBER

STUFFED RED PEPPERS

YIELD: 8 STUFFED
PEPPERS, 4 SERVINGS
PREP TIME: 20 MINUTES
COOK TIME: 18 TO
20 MINUTES

INGREDIENTS

2 tablespoons (30 ml) avocado oil

⅓ yellow onion, diced

1 jalapeño, diced

1 pound (454 g) ground beef

2 teaspoons (4 g) ground cumin

2 teaspoons (6 g) chili powder

2¼ teaspoons (6 g) garlic
  powder, divided

1 ounce (28 g) crushed pork rinds
  or almond flour

1¼ teaspoons (8 g) salt, divided

1 cup (113 g) precooked
  cauliflower rice

½ cup (120 ml) sugar-free marinara
  sauce (e.g., Rao's)

4 red bell peppers

½ cup (60 g) shredded mozzarella

NUTRITION: 1 SERVING = 2 STUFFED PEPPERS
CALORIES 413 KCAL
CARBOHYDRATE 14.3 G
TOTAL FAT 23.7 G
SATURATED FAT 8.1 G
TRANS FATS 0.9 G
SODIUM 1060.5 MG
TOTAL SUGARS 7.7 G
PROTEIN 36.5 G
FIBER 4.6 G

INSTRUCTIONS

1. Heat the avocado oil in a sauté pan over medium heat. Add the onion and jalapeño and on cook until the onion is translucent, about 3 minutes.

2. Add the ground beef, cumin and chili powder, 2 teaspoons (6 g) of the garlic powder, the pork rinds, and 1 teaspoon of the salt. Stir occasionally to cook evenly, breaking up larger pieces of beef with a wooden spoon, until cooked through, 5 to 10 minutes.

3. Add the precooked cauliflower rice and marinara sauce to the pan and stir to incorporate. Allow the mixture to simmer while you complete the next steps.

4. Cut the bell peppers in half lengthwise. Remove and discard the ribs and seeds. Sprinkle the remaining ¼ teaspoon salt and ¼ teaspoon garlic powder evenly inside all of the bell pepper halves.

5. Divide the ground beef filling among the pepper halves and top with the mozzarella cheese.

6. Place the peppers on the lower rack (it's okay if they're touching, but the cheese might melt together) and air-fry them at 350°F (180°C) for 8 to 10 minutes. The cheese should be golden brown and the bell pepper should be tender.

7. Carefully remove the peppers from the air fryer and serve immediately.

9.4 G NET CARBS = 13.1 G CARBOHYDRATES - 3.7 G FIBER

TACO ZUCCHINI BOATS

YIELD: 4 ZUCCHINI BOATS
PREP TIME: 15 TO
20 MINUTES
COOK TIME: 17 TO
19 MINUTES

INGREDIENTS

2 zucchinis

1 tablespoon (15 ml) avocado oil, plus more for brushing

1 teaspoon (6 g) salt, plus more for seasoning

⅓ yellow onion, diced

1 jalapeño, diced

1 pound (454 g) ground beef

2 teaspoons (4 g) ground cumin

2 teaspoons (6 g) chili powder

2 teaspoons (6 g) garlic powder

1 cup (113 g) precooked cauliflower rice

½ cup (120 ml) sugar-free marinara sauce (e.g., Rao's)

1 ounce (28 g) crushed pork rinds or almond flour

½ cup (60 g) shredded mozzarella

NUTRITION: 1 SERVING = 1 BOAT
CALORIES 442.2 KCAL
CARBOHYDRATE 13.1 G
TOTAL FAT 26 G
SATURATED FAT 9.4 G
TRANS FATS 1 G
SODIUM 994.6 MG
TOTAL SUGARS 7 G
PROTEIN 39.8 G
FIBER 3.7 G

INSTRUCTIONS

1. Trim the ends of the zucchinis and cut them lengthwise. Then scrape out the seeds to hollow them out into boats. Brush the flesh side with the avocado oil and season each piece with a pinch of salt.

2. Place the boats flesh-side up in the air fryer and air-fry them for 12 minutes at 375°F (190°C).

3. While the zucchini is cooking, heat the avocado oil in a sauté pan over medium heat. Add the onion and jalapeño and cook until the onion is translucent, about 3 minutes.

4. Add the ground beef, cumin, chili powder, garlic powder, and salt. Stir occasionally to cook evenly, breaking up larger pieces of beef with a wooden spoon, until the beef is cooked through, 5 to 10 minutes.

5. Add the cooked cauliflower and marinara sauce to the meat mixture and stir to combine.

6. Remove the zucchini boats from the air fryer and fill them with the meat mixture. Sprinkle with the pork rinds and then top with the cheese.

7. Air-fry the boats at 375°F (190°C) for 5 to 7 minutes, or until the cheese is golden brown. Remove them carefully and serve immediately.

TACO HAND PIES

YIELD: 4 HAND PIES
PREP TIME: 20 MINUTES
COOK TIME: 20 MINUTES

INGREDIENTS

2 tablespoons (30 ml) avocado oil

⅓ yellow onion, diced

1 jalapeño, diced

1 pound (454 g) ground beef

2 teaspoons (4 g) ground cumin

2 teaspoons (6 g) chili powder

2 teaspoons (6 g) garlic powder

1 teaspoon (6 g) salt

1 recipe Savory Protein Dough (page 129)

1 ounce (28 g) crushed pork rinds or almond flour

TIP: USE THE CONVECTION/BAKE SETTING IF YOUR AIR FRYER HAS IT. THIS WILL MEAN YOU DON'T HAVE TO FLIP THE HAND PIES.

NUTRITION: 1 SERVING = 1 HAND PIE
CALORIES 447.9 KCAL
CARBOHYDRATE 6.4 G
TOTAL FAT 29.1 G
SATURATED FAT 10.5 G
TRANS FATS 1 G
SODIUM 1085.2 MG
TOTAL SUGARS 2.1 G
PROTEIN 39.4 G
FIBER 1.4 G

INSTRUCTIONS

1. Heat the avocado oil in a pan over medium heat. Cook the onion and jalapeño in it until the onion is translucent, about 3 minutes.

2. Add the ground beef, seasonings, and salt. Stir occasionally to cook evenly, breaking up larger pieces of beef, until cooked through.

3. Meanwhile, divide the dough into 4 even pieces. Place each portion in between two sheets of parchment paper. Use a rolling pin or meat press to roll the dough out to a ½-inch (1.3 cm) thick disk.

4. Add 2 tablespoons (30 g) of filling to one side of the dough round and fold it over, crimping and sealing the edges with a fork. Repeat this process for all the hand pies.

5. Line the air fryer basket with parchment paper or greased foil. Place the hand pies in the basket and air-fry them at 350°F (180°C) for 6 minutes, or until the top is golden brown.

6. Flip the hand pies over and remove the parchment paper. Air-fry them for an additional 5 minutes, or until they are golden brown on the second side.

7. Remove the hand pies from the air fryer and allow them to cool for 5 minutes before serving.

2.4 G NET CARBS = 2.4 G CARBOHYDRATES - 0 G FIBER

TERIYAKI STEAK BITES

YIELD: **4 SERVINGS**
PREP TIME: **15 MINUTES +**
1 HOUR MARINATING
COOK TIME: **6 TO**
10 MINUTES

INGREDIENTS

- 1 pound (454 g) stew meat or sirloin steak
- 1 teaspoon (6 g) salt
- ¼ cup (60 ml) Teriyaki Marinade (page 146)

INSTRUCTIONS

1. Cut the steak into 1-inch (2.5 cm) cubes. Place them in a large plastic bag or baking pan, sprinkle them with the salt, and cover them with the marinade. Make sure the marinade coats the meat evenly. Allow the steak to marinate for at least 1 hour in the refrigerator.

2. Air-fry the steak cubes at 450°F (230°C) for 6 to 10 minutes, until they reach your desired doneness.

3. Remove the steak cubes and serve immediately, as is or with cauliflower rice.

NUTRITION: 1 SERVING = ¼ RECIPE
CALORIES 196.5 KCAL
CARBOHYDRATE 2.4 G
TOTAL FAT 5.4 G
SATURATED FAT 1.9 G
TRANS FATS 0.2 G
SODIUM 883.6 MG
TOTAL SUGARS 2.3 G
PROTEIN 34 G
FIBER 0 G

TACO PIE EGG CUPS

YIELD: 24 EGG CUPS
PREP TIME: 20 MINUTES
COOK TIME: 16 TO
18 MINUTES

INGREDIENTS

1 tablespoon (15 ml) avocado oil

1 yellow onion, diced

1 jalapeño, diced

2 pounds (908 g) ground beef

1 pound (454 g) ground pork

2 tablespoons (12 g) ground cumin

2 tablespoons (16 g) chili powder

2 tablespoons (20 g) garlic powder

1 tablespoon (18 g) salt

12 eggs

1 cup (240 g) sour cream

½ cup (60 g) shredded
   cheddar cheese

Silicone muffin liners

INSTRUCTIONS

1. Heat the avocado oil in a sauté pan over medium heat. Add the onion and jalapeño and cook until the onion is translucent, 4 to 5 minutes.

2. Add the ground beef and pork to the pan and break it apart to distribute it. Add the cumin, chili powder, garlic powder, and salt. Stir occasionally to cook evenly, breaking up larger pieces of beef with a wooden spoon, until it is cooked through, 5 to 10 minutes.

3. While the meat is cooking, in a large bowl, whisk the eggs and sour cream until they are a creamy yellow mixture.

4. Arrange as many silicone muffin liners as will fit in your air fryer tray. Fill them two-thirds with the meat mixture and one-third with the egg mixture. Top with the cheddar cheese.

5. Air-fry the egg cups at 350°F (180°C) for 6 to 8 minutes, or until the egg is set on the bottom. The tops might get a little bit brown.

6. Allow the egg cups to cool for 5 minutes on a drying rack and serve them warm or cold (like a quiche).

NUTRITION: 1 SERVING = 1 CUP
CALORIES 220.2 KCAL
CARBOHYDRATE 1.4 G
TOTAL FAT 15 G
SATURATED FAT 5.9 G
TRANS FATS 0.5 G
SODIUM 227.2 MG
TOTAL SUGARS 0.6 G
PROTEIN 19 G
FIBER 0.2 G

STAR INGREDIENT
CHICKEN

ADOBO CHICKEN QUARTERS

YIELD: **4** SERVINGS

PREP TIME: **6** TO **10** MINUTES

COOK TIME: **22** TO **25** MINUTES

INGREDIENTS

4 chicken leg quarters

1 tablespoon (15 ml) avocado oil

2 teaspoons (6 g) Adobo Seasoning (page 153)

INSTRUCTIONS

1. Pat both sides of the chicken skin dry with a paper towel or clean kitchen towel. Use your hands to coat the chicken evenly with the avocado oil and then season both sides with the adobo seasoning.

2. Grease the air fryer rack (or use greased foil or parchment paper if your air fryer cautions against greasing the rack). Place the chicken on the rack skin-side up.

3. Air-fry the chicken at 350°F (180°C) for 22 to 25 minutes, or until the internal temperature reaches 165°F (74°C) when checked with a meat thermometer.

4. Remove the chicken from the air fryer and allow it to rest for 8 minutes before serving.

NUTRITION: 1 SERVING = 1 CHICKEN LEG QUARTER
CALORIES 420.1 KCAL
CARBOHYDRATE 0 G
TOTAL FAT 30.4 G
SATURATED FAT 8.4 G
TRANS FATS 0 G
SODIUM 850 MG
TOTAL SUGARS 0 G
PROTEIN 34 G
FIBER 0 G

CHICKEN MARGARITA

YIELD: 4 SERVINGS
PREP TIME: 15 TO
20 MINUTES, PLUS 1 HOUR+
FOR MARINADE
COOK TIME: 25 MINUTES

INGREDIENTS

½ cup (75 g) halved cherry
  tomatoes or sliced Roma tomato
1 tablespoon (15 ml) lemon juice
4 boneless skinless chicken breasts
2 tablespoons (30 ml) avocado oil
1 tablespoon (15 ml)
  balsamic vinegar
1 teaspoon (6 g) salt
1 teaspoon (3 g) garlic powder
1 teaspoon (1 g) Italian seasoning
½ teaspoon red pepper flakes
½ cup (120 ml) keto-friendly pesto
  (e.g., Rao's)
4 slices mozzarella cheese

TIP: MARINATE THE CHICKEN FOR UP TO AN
HOUR TO REALLY INCORPORATE THE FLAVORS.

NUTRITION: 1 SERVING
CALORIES 350.2 KCAL
CARBOHYDRATE 3.8 G
TOTAL FAT 24.7 G
SATURATED FAT 6.9 G
TRANS FATS 0.1 G
SODIUM 1015.7 MG
TOTAL SUGARS 1.6 G
PROTEIN 26.3 G
FIBER 0.7

INSTRUCTIONS

1. In a small bowl, combine the tomatoes and lemon juice and set aside.

2. Butterfly the chicken breasts. Open the chicken and place it in a plastic bag. Use a meat tenderizer or rolling pin to flatten out the chicken until it is about ¼ inch (6 mm) thick. Set aside.

3. In a large bowl, combine the avocado oil, balsamic vinegar, salt, garlic powder, Italian seasoning, and red pepper flakes. Whisk to blend and then add the butterflied chicken breasts. Turn to coat them in the marinade.

4. Remove the chicken from the marinade and place it on the top rack of your air fryer, open-side down. Air-fry it at 350°F (180°C) for 8 minutes.

5. Flip the chicken over and smear the pesto on the inside of it. Top it with the tomatoes and a slice of mozzarella cheese.

6. Increase the temperature of your air fryer to 450°F (230°C) and cook the chicken for 2 to 4 minutes longer, until the mozzarella is golden brown and the chicken has reached an internal temperature of 165°F (74°C) when checked with a meat thermometer.

7. The chicken and tomatoes will be juicy, so remove them carefully with a broad spoon or spatula and serve immediately.

5.3 G NET CARBS = 6.6 G CARBOHYDRATES - 1.3 G FIBER

BUFFALO CHICKEN HAND PIES

YIELD: 4 HAND PIES
PREP TIME: 15 TO
20 MINUTES
COOK TIME: 20 MINUTES

INGREDIENTS

2 tablespoons (30 ml) avocado oil

1 yellow onion, diced

1 jalapeño, diced

8 ounces (227 g) cooked and shredded chicken

¼ cup (60 ml) your favorite keto-friendly hot sauce

½ teaspoon garlic powder

⅛ teaspoon cayenne pepper

2 ounces (56 g) cream cheese, at room temperature

1 tablespoon (14 g) unsalted butter

1 recipe Savory Protein Dough (page 129)

TIP: USE THE CONVECTION/BAKE SETTING IF YOUR AIR FRYER HAS IT. THIS WILL MEAN YOU DON'T NEED TO FLIP THE HAND PIES.

NUTRITION: 1 SERVING = 1 HAND PIE
CALORIES 452.1 KCAL
CARBOHYDRATE 6.6 G
TOTAL FAT 32.7 G
SATURATED FAT 14.9 G
TRANS FATS 0.7 G
SODIUM 1915.5 MG
TOTAL SUGARS 1.8 G
PROTEIN 34.4 G
FIBER 1.3 G

INSTRUCTIONS

1. Heat the avocado oil in a sauté pan over medium heat. Add the onion and jalapeño and cook until the onion is translucent, 3 to 4 minutes.

2. Add the shredded chicken, hot sauce, garlic powder, and cayenne pepper. Decrease the heat to medium-low and add the cream cheese. Stir to combine. Add the butter and stir to combine until it is entirely melted.

3. Divide the dough into 4 portions and place each on a piece of parchment. Cover them with another piece of parchment. Use a rolling pin or meat press to roll out the dough to a ½-inch (1.3 cm) thick disk.

4. Place 2 tablespoons (30 g) of filling on one side and fold the dough over, pressing the edges with a fork to crimp and seal them. Repeat this process for all the hand pies.

5. Line the air fryer basket with parchment paper or greased foil and place the hand pies on top. Air-fry the hand pies at 350°F (180°C) for 6 minutes, or until the top is golden brown.

6. Flip the hand pies over and remove the parchment paper. Air-fry them for an additional 5 minutes, or until golden brown.

7. Carefully remove the hand pies from the air fryer and allow to cool for 5 minutes before serving.

COCONUT CURRY CHICKEN

YIELD: 4 SERVINGS
PREP TIME: 10 MINUTES
COOK TIME: 8 MINUTES

INGREDIENTS

4 boneless skinless chicken breasts

2 teaspoons (10 ml) avocado oil

1 teaspoon (6 g) salt

¾ teaspoon garam masala

¼ teaspoon curry powder

¼ teaspoon ginger powder

¼ teaspoon smoked paprika

1 recipe Coconut Curry Peanut Sauce (page 135)

INSTRUCTIONS

1. Cut the chicken into thin strips and pat dry with paper towels.

2. In a medium-size bowl, combine the avocado oil, salt, garam marsala, curry powder, ginger powder, and smoked paprika. Whisk to blend.

3. Add the chicken strips to the bowl and toss to combine. Make sure the chicken strips are fully covered.

4. Place the chicken strips in the air fryer basket and air-fry them at 350°F (180°C) for 8 minutes, or until there's no pink inside and the chicken has reached an internal temperature of 165°F (74°C) when checked with a meat thermometer.

5. Allow the chicken strips to cool and set for 5 minutes, and then coat them with the sauce.

NUTRITION: 1 SERVING = ¼ RECIPE
CALORIES 307.1 KCAL
CARBOHYDRATE 4.5 G
TOTAL FAT 21.2 G
SATURATED FAT 13.6 G
TRANS FATS 0 G
SODIUM 1130.1 MG
TOTAL SUGARS 2.4 G
PROTEIN 21.6 G
FIBER 1 G

BUFFALO CHICKEN ZUCCHINI BOATS

YIELD: **4 ZUCCHINI BOATS**
PREP TIME: 18 TO
20 MINUTES
COOK TIME: 20 MINUTES

INGREDIENTS

2 zucchinis

Avocado oil spray

Salt, to taste

8 ounces (227 g) cooked and shredded chicken

2 ounces (56 g) cream cheese

¼ cup (60 ml) your favorite keto-friendly hot sauce (e.g., Frank's)

1 tablespoon (14 g) unsalted butter

½ teaspoon garlic powder

⅛ teaspoon cayenne pepper

½ cup (60 g) shredded cheddar cheese

INSTRUCTIONS

1. Trim the ends of the zucchinis and cut them in half lengthwise. Scrape out the seeds to make hollowed-out boats. Spray the flesh sides with avocado oil and sprinkle with a pinch of salt.

2. Air-fry the boats at 375°F (190°C) for 12 minutes.

3. While the zucchini is cooking, combine the chicken, cream cheese, hot sauce, butter, garlic powder, and cayenne pepper in a saucepan over medium-low heat. Stir to combine until the cream cheese is softened.

4. Remove the zucchini boats from the air fryer and fill them with the chicken mixture. Top with the shredded cheese.

5. Return the filled boats to the air fryer and air-fry them at 375°F (190°C) for 5 to 7 minutes longer, or until the cheese is golden brown.

6. Remove the boats carefully and serve immediately.

NUTRITION: 1 SERVING = 1 ZUCCHINI BOAT
CALORIES 212.8 KCAL
CARBOHYDRATE 4.7 G
TOTAL FAT 13.8 G
SATURATED FAT 8.3 G
TRANS FATS 0.3 G
SODIUM 1260.6 MG
TOTAL SUGARS 3 G
PROTEIN 18.2 G
FIBER 1 G

CHICKEN PARMESAN

YIELD: 4 SERVINGS
PREP TIME: 15 TO
20 MINUTES
COOK TIME: 25 MINUTES

INGREDIENTS

4 boneless skinless chicken breasts
½ teaspoon salt, plus more
   for sprinkling
1 large egg
1 recipe Crumb Coating (page 152)
1 tablespoon (3.6 g)
   Italian seasoning
½ cup (120 ml) sugar-free marinara
   sauce (e.g., Rao's)
4 slices fresh mozzarella cheese
¼ cup (25 g) grated
   Parmesan cheese

INSTRUCTIONS

1. To butterfly a chicken breast, place one hand on the top of the chicken and slice it nearly in half. Open up the chicken and place it in a plastic bag. Use a meat tenderizer or a rolling pin to flatten out the chicken until it is about ¼ inch (6 mm) thick. Sprinkle both sides of the chicken with salt.

2. Grease the air fryer basket (or use greased foil or parchment paper if your air fryer cautions against greasing the rack).

3. Beat the egg in a medium-size shallow baking dish and add a splash of water to make an egg wash.

4. In a second shallow dish, combine the crumb coating, Italian seasoning, and salt.

5. Dip each butterflied chicken in the egg wash, and then in the crumb coating, covering the chicken completely and pressing it firmly to adhere. You might have to cut the chicken into smaller pieces to fit the dish.

6. Place the chicken on the top rack and air-fry it at 350°F (180°C) for 8 minutes. Try to make sure the chicken isn't layered too much, but if you need to for this step, that's okay.

NUTRITION: 1 SERVING = 1 CHICKEN BREAST
CALORIES 256.1 KCAL
CARBOHYDRATE 1.4 G
TOTAL FAT 13.7 G
SATURATED FAT 6 G
TRANS FATS 0 G
SODIUM 925.1 MG
TOTAL SUGARS 0.8 G
PROTEIN 29.1 G
FIBER 0 G

7. While the chicken is cooking, warm the marinara sauce in a small pot over low heat; this should take about 10 minutes.

8. Flip the chicken and air-fry it for 3 minutes longer. It is still okay if the chicken breasts are layered or touching.

9. Top each breast with a slice of fresh mozzarella and sprinkle with the Parmesan cheese. Sprinkle with salt. At this point, try to make sure they're not touching or layered.

10. Increase the temperature to 450°F (230°C) and cook the chicken for 2 to 4 minutes longer, until the cheese is golden brown and the chicken has reached an internal temperature of 165°F (74°C) when checked with a meat thermometer.

11. Top the chicken with the warm marinara sauce and serve immediately.

GREEK CHICKEN QUARTERS

YIELD: 4 SERVINGS
PREP TIME: 15 MINUTES +
1 HOUR MARINATING
COOK TIME: 22 TO
25 MINUTES

INGREDIENTS

4 chicken leg quarters
1 teaspoon (6 g) salt
1 recipe Greek Dressing and
  Marinade (page 141)

INSTRUCTIONS

1. Pat the chicken dry with a paper towel and season it with salt on both sides.

2. Place the chicken in a large plastic resealable bag or baking pan and pour the Greek dressing over it. Turn to coat it in the dressing. Refrigerate it for 1 hour.

3. Remove the chicken from the marinade. Place it on the rack skin-side up. Air-fry it at 350°F (180°C) for 22 to 25 minutes, or until the internal temperature reaches 165°F (74°C) when checked with a meat thermometer.

4. Remove carefully from the air fryer and allow it to rest for 10 minutes.

TIP: YOU CAN MARINATE THESE FOR A DAY OR LONGER IF YOU COVER THE CHICKEN IN THE FRIDGE. THESE ARE GREAT FOR ENTERTAINING ON A WEEKNIGHT OR JUST TO ENJOY FOR YOURSELF. SHRED THE LEFTOVERS TO USE IN OTHER RECIPES, SUCH AS THE BUFFALO CHICKEN ZUCCHINI BOATS ON PAGE 62.

NUTRITION: 1 SERVING = 1 CHICKEN LEG QUARTER
CALORIES 516.5 KCAL
CARBOHYDRATE 1 G
TOTAL FAT 40.7 G
SATURATED FAT 9.6 G
TRANS FATS 0 G
SODIUM 770.4 MG
TOTAL SUGARS 0.1 G
PROTEIN 34.2 G
FIBER 0.3 G

CHICKEN TIKKA MASALA MEATBALLS

YIELD: 20 MEATBALLS,
4 SERVINGS
PREP TIME: 15 MINUTES
COOK TIME: 8 MINUTES

INGREDIENTS

1 pound (454 g) ground chicken or ground turkey

1 egg, lightly beaten

½ cup (15 g) ground pork rinds

1 teaspoon (7 g) grated fresh ginger

2 cloves garlic, minced

2 tablespoons (2 g) chopped cilantro

1 tablespoon (15 g) keto-friendly tomato paste

1 tablespoon (5 g) garam masala

1 teaspoon (2 g) onion powder

1 teaspoon (6 g) salt

1 recipe Tikka Masala Sauce (page 147)

INSTRUCTIONS

1. Place the chicken, egg, pork rinds, ginger, garlic, cilantro, tomato paste, garam masala, onion powder, and salt in a large bowl. With clean hands, knead everything to evenly distribute the ingredients.

2. Grease a wire air fryer rack (or use greased foil or parchment paper if your air fryer cautions against greasing the rack).

3. Use a small cookie scoop to make 20 meatballs and place them in your air fryer. They will cook best if they're close but not touching, so you may have to air-fry them in batches.

4. Air-fry the meatballs at 400°F (200°C) for 8 minutes. If you are using parchment paper, flip the meatballs over halfway through.

5. Transfer the meatballs to a large bowl, add the tikka masala sauce, and toss to coat.

NUTRITION: 1 SERVING = 5 MEATBALLS
CALORIES 391.6 KCAL
CARBOHYDRATE 5.4 G
TOTAL FAT 27.1 G
SATURATED FAT 15.3 G
TRANS FATS 0.1 G
SODIUM 927 MG
TOTAL SUGARS 1.9 G
PROTEIN 31.6 G
FIBER 1.1 G

CRISPY CHICKEN TENDERS

YIELD: 4 SERVINGS

PREP TIME: 10 MINUTES +
3 TO 12 HOURS MARINATING

COOK TIME: 10 TO
15 MINUTES

INGREDIENTS

1 pound (454 g) chicken tenders

½ cup (120 ml) pickle juice

1 teaspoon (5 ml) your favorite keto-friendly hot sauce (e.g., Frank's)

½ teaspoon salt

1 large egg

1 recipe Crumb Coating (page 152)

½ teaspoon chili powder

1 recipe Everything Sauce (page 138)

INSTRUCTIONS

1. In a bag or bowl, combine the chicken tenders, pickle juice, and hot sauce. Refrigerate for at least 3 hours or overnight.

2. Remove the chicken tenders from the marinade and lay them out on a large plate or baking mat. Sprinkle both sides with the salt.

3. Grease the air fryer tray (or use greased foil or parchment paper if your air fryer cautions against greasing the rack).

4. Beat the egg in a medium-size shallow baking dish and add a splash of water to make an egg wash.

5. In a second shallow dish, stir the crumb coating and chili powder to combine.

6. Dip each chicken tender into the egg wash, and then in the crumb coating, covering it completely and firmly pressing the crumb mixture into the chicken to adhere.

7. Arrange the chicken tenders on the top rack. It's okay if they're touching but better if they're not. Air-fry them at 350°F (180°C) for 8 minutes.

8. Flip the tenders over and cook for 2 to 4 minutes longer, until the chicken is crispy and has reached an internal temperature of 165°F (74°C) when checked with a meat thermometer. Serve it with the sauce.

NUTRITION: 1 SERVING = ¼ RECIPE
CALORIES 161.8 KCAL
CARBOHYDRATE 0.4 G
TOTAL FAT 4.5 G
SATURATED FAT 1.2 G
TRANS FATS 0 G
SODIUM 482.8 MG
TOTAL SUGARS 0 G
PROTEIN 31.3 G
FIBER 0 G

GENERAL TSO CHICKEN

YIELD: 4 SERVINGS
PREP TIME: 15 MINUTES
COOK TIME: 10 MINUTES

INGREDIENTS

1 pound (454 g) chicken tenders, breasts, or thighs

½ teaspoon salt

1 large egg

1 recipe Crumb Coating (page 152)

½ teaspoon chili powder

1 recipe General Tso Sauce (page 140)

INSTRUCTIONS

1. Cut the chicken into bite-size pieces. Sprinkle both sides with the salt.

2. Grease the air fryer rack (or use greased foil or parchment paper if your air fryer cautions against greasing the rack).

3. Beat the egg in a medium-size shallow baking dish and add a splash of water to make an egg wash.

4. In a second shallow dish, combine the crumb coating and chili powder.

5. Dip each piece of chicken into the egg wash and then into the crumb coating, covering it completely and firmly pressing the coating into the chicken to adhere.

6. Arrange the chicken pieces on the top rack; it's okay if they're touching but they will be crispier if they're not.

7. Air-fry the chicken at 350°F (180°C) for 5 minutes per side, or until it is crispy.

8. Transfer the chicken to a medium-size bowl and add the sauce, tossing to combine.

NUTRITION: 1 SERVING = ¼ RECIPE
CALORIES 204.5 KCAL
CARBOHYDRATE 3.6 G
TOTAL FAT 7.1 G
SATURATED FAT 1.6 G
TRANS FATS 0 G
SODIUM 787.6 MG
TOTAL SUGARS 2.9 G
PROTEIN 31.8 G
FIBER 0.1 G

RANCH CHICKEN BREAST

YIELD: 4 SERVINGS

PREP TIME: 6 MINUTES

COOK TIME: 15 TO 17 MINUTES

INGREDIENTS

4 boneless skinless chicken breasts

1 tablespoon (15 ml) avocado oil

1 teaspoon (6 g) salt

½ teaspoon garlic powder

½ cup (120 g) cream cheese, softened

2 teaspoons (6 g) Ranch Seasoning (page 155)

INSTRUCTIONS

1. Butterfly the chicken breasts: Open the chicken up and place it in a plastic bag. Use a meat tenderizer or rolling pin to flatten the chicken until it is about ¼ inch (6 mm) thick.

2. Brush the chicken with the avocado oil and sprinkle both sides with the salt and garlic powder.

3. Grease the air fryer rack (or use greased foil or parchment paper if your air fryer cautions against greasing the rack).

4. Place the butterflied chicken on the rack with the inside (cut side) facing up. Air-fry it at 350°F (180°C) for 7 minutes.

5. In a small bowl, combine the softened cream cheese with the ranch seasoning, using a fork to loosen up the cream cheese.

6. Remove the chicken from the air fryer and flip it over. Top it with the cream cheese mixture and return it to the air fryer.

7. Air-fry the chicken at 400°F (200°C) for 3 to 5 minutes, or until the topping is golden brown and the chicken reaches an internal temperature of 165°F (74°C).

8. Remove the chicken carefully from the air fryer and allow it to rest for 5 minutes.

NUTRITION: 1 SERVING = 1 CHICKEN BREAST
CALORIES 233.8 KCAL
CARBOHYDRATE 2.1 G
TOTAL FAT 15.4 G
SATURATED FAT 6.6 G
TRANS FATS 0.3 G
SODIUM 717.7 MG
TOTAL SUGARS 1.1 G
PROTEIN 21 G
FIBER 0.1 G

SPINACH ARTICHOKE CHICKEN

YIELD: **4 SERVINGS**

PREP TIME: **7 MINUTES**

COOK TIME: **10 TO 12 MINUTES**

INGREDIENTS

4 boneless skinless chicken breasts

1 tablespoon (15 ml) avocado oil

1 teaspoon (6 g) salt

½ teaspoon garlic powder

½ cup (120 g) spinach artichoke dip

INSTRUCTIONS

1. To butterfly a chicken breast, place one hand on the top of the chicken and slice the chicken nearly in half. Open the chicken up and place it in a plastic bag. Use a meat tenderizer or rolling pin to flatten out the chicken until it is about ¼ inch (6 mm) thick.

2. Brush the chicken with the avocado oil and sprinkle both sides with the salt and garlic powder, rubbing the spices into the chicken.

3. Place the chicken the on air fryer rack cut-side up. Air-fry it at 350°F (180°C) for 7 minutes.

4. Carefully flip the chicken and smear the spinach artichoke dip on top.

5. Air-fry the chicken at 400°F (200°C) for 3 to 5 minutes, or until the topping is golden brown.

NUTRITION: 1 SERVING = 1 CHICKEN BREAST
CALORIES 216.7 KCAL
CARBOHYDRATE 2.3 G
TOTAL FAT 12.7 G
SATURATED FAT 2.9 G
TRANS FATS 0.1 G
SODIUM 796.2 MG
TOTAL SUGARS 0.3 G
PROTEIN 22.4 G
FIBER 0.7 G

SESAME CHICKEN

YIELD: **4 SERVINGS**
PREP TIME: **15 MINUTES**
COOK TIME: **10 MINUTES**

INGREDIENTS

1 pound (454 g) boneless chicken tenders, breast, or thighs

½ teaspoon salt

1 large egg

1 recipe Crumb Coating (page 152)

½ teaspoon red pepper flakes

1 recipe Sesame Sauce (page 144)

2 tablespoons (16 g) sesame seeds, for serving (optional)

2 tablespoons (10 g) sliced scallion, for serving (optional)

INSTRUCTIONS

1. Pat the chicken dry and cut it into 1-inch (2.5 cm) cubes. Transfer them to a medium-size bowl. Season with the salt.

2. Grease the air fryer rack (or use greased foil or parchment paper if your air fryer cautions against greasing the rack).

3. Beat the egg in a medium-size shallow baking dish and add a splash of water to make an egg wash.

4. In a second shallow dish, stir the crumb coating and red pepper flakes to combine.

5. Dip each chicken piece into the egg wash and then into the crumb coating, covering it completely and pressing firmly to adhere.

6. Arrange the chicken pieces on the top rack. It's okay if they touch but they shouldn't be too crowded. Air-fry them at 350°F (180°C) for 5 minutes, flipping them halfway through so that both sides are crispy.

7. Transfer the chicken bites to a large bowl. Pour the sauce over them and toss to coat.

8. Sprinkle the chicken with the sesame seeds and scallion, if desired.

NUTRITION: 1 SERVING = ¼ RECIPE
CALORIES 249.3 KCAL
CARBOHYDRATE 5.3 G
TOTAL FAT 11.3 G
SATURATED FAT 2.2 G
TRANS FATS 0 G
SODIUM 981.2 MG
TOTAL SUGARS 4.5 G
PROTEIN 31.6 G
FIBER 0.3 G

TUSCAN CHICKEN THIGHS

YIELD: 4 SERVINGS

PREP TIME: 10 TO 12 MINUTES

COOK TIME: 16 TO 17 MINUTES

INGREDIENTS

1 pound (454 g) chicken thighs

2 tablespoons (30 ml) avocado oil

½ teaspoon salt

½ cup (75 g) cherry tomatoes

¾ cup (180 ml) heavy cream

¾ cup (180 ml) chicken broth

1 tablespoon (15 ml) mustard

1 teaspoon (3 g) garlic powder

1 tablespoon (3.6 g) Italian seasoning

1 teaspoon (5 ml) lemon juice

½ cup (50 g) grated Parmesan cheese

1 cup (30 g) baby spinach

1 tablespoon (4 g) julienned basil

INSTRUCTIONS

1. Pat the chicken thighs dry with a paper towel. Massage the chicken thighs with the oil and season them all over with the salt.

2. Air-fry the chicken at 400°F (200°C) for 7 minutes.

3. Flip the chicken over and add the cherry tomatoes on top. Air-fry it for 7 minutes longer.

4. While the chicken is cooking, combine the heavy cream, chicken broth, mustard, garlic powder, Italian seasoning, and lemon juice in a skillet over medium-low heat. Whisk to combine. When the mixture starts to bubble, add the Parmesan cheese bit by bit until the sauce starts to thicken.

5. Add the spinach and reduce the heat to a simmer. Cook another 2 to 3 minutes, or until the spinach wilts (make sure the temperature isn't too high or the sauce will burn).

6. Remove the chicken and the cherry tomatoes from the air fryer with a spoon and add them to the pot with the sauce. Ladle the sauce over the chicken and top with the basil. Cook for 2 to 3 minutes to blend the flavors.

NUTRITION: 1 SERVING = ¼ RECIPE
CALORIES 382.1 KCAL
CARBOHYDRATE 6 G
TOTAL FAT 22.5 G
SATURATED FAT 8 G
TRANS FATS 0.4 G
SODIUM 701.6 MG
TOTAL SUGARS 2.6 G
PROTEIN 37.9 G
FIBER 0.6 G

STAR INGREDIENT
PORK

CHICKEN SKIN WONTONS **78**

CRISPY BONELESS PORK LOIN CHOPS **79**

HAM AND CHEDDAR PINWHEELS **80**

PORK BELLY **82**

TERIYAKI PORK TENDERLOIN **83**

SCOTCH EGGS **84**

CHICKEN SKIN WONTONS

YIELD: 6 SERVINGS
PREP TIME: 9 MINUTES
COOK TIME: 6 MINUTES

INGREDIENTS

¼ cup (60 ml) coconut aminos

2 tablespoons (30 ml) rice wine vinegar

1 tablespoon (8 g) ginger paste

2 teaspoons (10 ml) chili garlic sauce

2 teaspoons (12 g) salt, plus more as needed

1 teaspoon (5 ml) fish sauce

1 pound (454 g) ground pork

6 cloves garlic, minced

¼ cup (40 g) minced shallot

2 cups (140 g) shredded cabbage

6 tablespoons (30 g) sliced scallion

8 ounces (227 g) chicken skin, cut into 2-inch (5 cm) squares

1 teaspoon (5 ml) sesame oil

1 recipe Wonton Dipping Sauce (page 150)

NUTRITION: 1 SERVING
CALORIES 434.4 KCAL
CARBOHYDRATE 5.8 G
TOTAL FAT 32.3 G
SATURATED FAT 10.1 G
TRANS FATS 0.5 G
SODIUM 1173.7 MG
TOTAL SUGARS 3.7 G
PROTEIN 29.1 G
FIBER 1 G

INSTRUCTIONS

1. In a medium-size bowl, whisk the coconut aminos, rice wine vinegar, ginger paste, chili garlic sauce, salt, and fish sauce until fully combined. Set it aside.

2. In a large bowl, combine the ground pork, minced garlic, shallot, cabbage, and scallion. With clean hands, knead the mixture to evenly distribute the ingredients. Add the coconut aminos mixture and stir to combine.

3. Lay out the chicken skin wrappers. Place 1 tablespoon (15 g) of the filling in each. Fold it to close and pinch the seam to seal it. Add a pinch of salt to each wonton.

4. Grease the air fryer rack (or use greased foil or parchment paper if your air fryer cautions against greasing the rack). Place the wontons on the rack, seam-side down, and drizzle them with the sesame oil.

5. Air-fry the wontons at 400°F (200°C) for 3 minutes. Carefully flip them over and air-fry them for 3 minutes longer.

6. The wontons may be fragile, so take care when you remove them. Serve with the dipping sauce.

CRISPY BONELESS PORK LOIN CHOPS

YIELD: 4 SERVINGS
PREP TIME: 6 MINUTES
COOK TIME: 10 MINUTES

INGREDIENTS

1 large egg

1 teaspoon (5 ml) lemon juice

1 recipe Crumb Coating (page 152)

1 tablespoon (8 g) garlic powder

1 teaspoon (2 g) paprika

1 pound (454 g) boneless pork loin chops

INSTRUCTIONS

1. In a bowl large enough to fit the pork chops, beat the egg with the lemon juice.

2. On a plate, stir the crumb mixture, garlic powder, and paprika to combine.

3. Dip each pork chop in the egg wash and then coat it in the crumb mixture, pressing to adhere.

4. Grease the air fryer rack (or use greased foil or parchment paper if your air fryer cautions against greasing the rack). Place the chops on the rack.

5. Air-fry the chops at 350°F (180°C) for 7 minutes. Flip them over and air-fry for 3 minutes longer.

TIP: APPLES ARE NOT PART OF A KETO DIET (AND APPLESAUCE IS A STAPLE WITH MOST PORK CHOP DISHES), SO TRY THIS RECIPE WITH THE MOCK APPLE HAND PIES (PAGE 120) FOR A DELIGHTFUL DINNER.

NUTRITION: 1 SERVING
CALORIES 815.1 KCAL
CARBOHYDRATE 6.3 G
TOTAL FAT 30.6 G
SATURATED FAT 10.1 G
TRANS FATS 0.2 G
SODIUM 892.7 MG
TOTAL SUGARS 0.9 G
PROTEIN 122.4 G
FIBER 1 G

HAM AND CHEDDAR PINWHEELS

INGREDIENTS

1 recipe Savory Protein Dough (page 129)

6 slices ham

6 ounces (170 g) cheddar cheese (sliced or shredded)

INSTRUCTIONS

1. Lay out parchment paper and roll out the dough to ½ inch (1.3 cm) thick or less. Try to keep it in a rectangle shape so that the long edges are parallel and make for an easier roll.

2. Place the ham slices on top of the dough. It's okay if they're layered slightly. Place the cheddar on top. You can alternate the fillings if you like.

3. Gently pick up one of the long edges of the dough and roll the contents into a long tube-like spiral, using the parchment paper to help roll. Cut the roll into 24 even slices.

4. Grease a new piece of parchment paper or foil and lay the pinwheels on it filling-side up. Air-fry them at 350°F (180°C) for 3 to 4 minutes, or until the tops are golden brown.

5. Remove and serve the pinwheels immediately. Leftovers will keep in the fridge for up to a week.

TIP: IF YOU'RE NEW TO AIR-FRYING, PLAY AROUND WITH THE DIFFERENT SETTINGS! FOR THIS RECIPE IN PARTICULAR, YOU CAN USE THE CONVECTION OR BAKE SETTING IF YOUR AIR FRYER HAS IT. THIS RESULTS IN A CRISPIER BOTTOM.

NUTRITION: 1 SERVING = 6 PINWHEELS
CALORIES 432.9 KCAL
CARBOHYDRATE 24.2 G
TOTAL FAT 19 G
SATURATED FAT 5.2 G
TRANS FATS 0.1 G
SODIUM 75.4 MG
TOTAL SUGARS 1 G
PROTEIN 5.3 G
FIBER 0.2 G

PORK BELLY

YIELD: 4 SERVINGS
PREP TIME: 5 MINUTES
COOK TIME: 32 MINUTES

INGREDIENTS

1 pound (454 g) pork belly, cut into strips
1 teaspoon (6 g) salt

TIP: PORK BELLY IS BETTER THAN BACON AND JUST AS DELICIOUS. IT CAN BE INTIMIDATING TO WORK WITH AT FIRST AFTER THE EASE OF COOKING WITH BACON, BUT IT IS TOTALLY WORTH IT. COOKING TIME VARIES GREATLY BASED UPON THE THICKNESS OF THE PORK BELLY. THIS RECIPE USES 1-INCH (2.5 CM) THICK AND 10-INCH (25 CM) LONG STRIPS. IF YOU'RE FEELING REALLY ADVENTUROUS, YOU CAN MARINATE THE STRIPS IN COCONUT AMINOS FOR UP TO AN HOUR BEFOREHAND.

NUTRITION: 1 SERVING
CALORIES 587.4 KCAL
CARBOHYDRATE 0 G
TOTAL FAT 60.1 G
SATURATED FAT 21.9 G
TRANS FATS 0 G
SODIUM 625.7 MG
TOTAL SUGARS 0 G
PROTEIN 10.6 G
FIBER 0 G

INSTRUCTIONS

1. Pat the pork belly dry with a paper towel. Season both sides generously with the salt.

2. Place the pork belly strips in the basket. It's better if they're not touching (they'll get crispier that way), but you can layer them if necessary.

3. Air-fry the pork belly at 350°F (180°C) for 8 minutes and then flip the slices and continue to air-fry for 8 minutes longer.

4. Increase the air-fryer temperature to 450°F (230°C). Flip the slices back to the first side and air-fry for 8 minutes. Then flip the slices again and air-fry for 8 minutes longer. If the pork belly isn't done to your desired crispiness, cook it an additional 2 minutes, watching carefully.

5. Remove the strips from the air fryer and let them rest for 5 minutes.

6. Enjoy immediately. Leftovers will keep in the fridge for about a week.

TERIYAKI PORK TENDERLOIN

YIELD: 4 SERVINGS
PREP TIME: 7 MINUTES +
1 TO 9 HOURS FOR
MARINATING
COOK TIME: 16 TO
20 MINUTES

INGREDIENTS

1 pound (454 g) pork tenderloin
¼ cup (60 ml) Teriyaki Marinade (page 146)
1 tablespoon (15 ml) avocado oil
1 teaspoon (6 g) salt

INSTRUCTIONS

1. Combine the pork tenderloin, teriyaki marinade, avocado oil, and salt in a resealable plastic bag or in a baking dish with a lid. Cover the pork tenderloin completely and allow it to marinate for at least 1 hour and up to 9 hours in the refrigerator.

2. Grease the air fryer rack (or use greased foil or parchment paper if your air fryer cautions against greasing the rack).

3. Remove the tenderloin from the marinade. Place the tenderloin on the bottom rack and air-fry it at 400°F (200°C) for 8 to 10 minutes per side, or until the internal temperature reaches 145°F (63°C) when checked with a meat thermometer.

4. Remove the tenderloin from the air fryer and allow to rest 5 minutes.

5. Slice the tenderloin and serve it as is or with cauliflower rice.

NUTRITION: 1 SERVING
CALORIES 166.5 KCAL
CARBOHYDRATE 2.4 G
TOTAL FAT 5.2 G
SATURATED FAT 1.1 G
TRANS FATS 0 G
SODIUM 868.9 MG
TOTAL SUGARS 2.3 G
PROTEIN 25.2 G
FIBER 0 G

SCOTCH EGGS

YIELD: 12 EGGS
PREP TIME: 15 MINUTES
COOK TIME: 12 TO
16 MINUTES

INGREDIENTS

1 teaspoon (6 g)salt

1 teaspoon (1 g) dried thyme

½ teaspoon dried sage

½ teaspoon dried rosemary

½ teaspoon cayenne pepper

1 pound (454 g) ground pork

½ cup (15 g) Crumb Coating
   (page 152)

12 eggs, hard-boiled with a soft yolk

1 recipe Everything Sauce
   (page 138), for serving

INSTRUCTIONS

1. In a small bowl, whisk the salt, thyme, sage, rosemary, and cayenne pepper to make a spice mixture.

2. In a large bowl, combine the seasonings and ground pork. With clean hands, knead the mixture to evenly distribute the ingredients.

3. Place the crumb coating in a shallow dish. Grease the air fryer rack (or use greased foil or parchment paper if your air fryer cautions against greasing the rack).

4. Divide the pork mixture into 12 equal portions. Flatten each portion into a flat disk and wrap around an egg.

5. Roll each egg in the crumb coating and place it on the rack. The eggs can be close, but ideally they should not be touching too much.

6. Air-fry the eggs at 400°F (200°C) for 6 to 8 minutes. Flip them and air-fry them for 6 to 8 minutes longer.

7. Serve the eggs with the sauce and enjoy immediately. Scotch eggs will keep in the fridge for about 10 days.

NUTRITION: 1 SERVING = 1 EGG
CALORIES 200.8 KCAL
CARBOHYDRATE 0.8 G
TOTAL FAT 14 G
SATURATED FAT 4.7 G
TRANS FATS 0.1 G
SODIUM 317.4 MG
TOTAL SUGARS 0.6 G
PROTEIN 17.5 G
FIBER 0.1 G

STAR INGREDIENT
SEAFOOD

CAJUN SHRIMP 88

COCONUT CURRY SHRIMP 90

GARLIC BUTTER SHRIMP 91

COCONUT-CRUSTED SHRIMP 92

LEMON DILL SALMON 94

SPICY SCALLOPS 95

FISH CAKES 96

CAJUN SHRIMP

YIELD: 16 SHRIMP,
2 SERVINGS
PREP TIME: 5 MINUTES
COOK TIME: 5 MINUTES

INGREDIENTS

16 jumbo shrimp, peeled
and deveined

1 teaspoon (5 ml) avocado oil

1 teaspoon (1 g) Cajun Seasoning
(page 154)

¼ teaspoon salt

Lime wedges, for serving (optional)

INSTRUCTIONS

1. In a large bowl, toss the shrimp with the avocado oil. Add the Cajun seasoning and salt and toss to coat.

2. Place the shrimp on the air fryer rack. It's okay if the shrimp are touching as they won't get too crispy. Air-fry them at 400°F (200°C) for 5 minutes.

3. Serve with the lime wedges, if desired.

TIP: ONCE YOU'VE MADE THESE SHRIMP, YOU'LL FIND THAT THEY'RE SUPER VERSATILE. YOU CAN EAT THEM AS IS AS A KIND OF SHRIMP COCKTAIL OR ADD THEM TO A LETTUCE WRAP WITH CRUNCHY VEGGIES IF YOU'RE LOOKING FOR SOMETHING FRESHER. IF YOU'RE NOT SURE ABOUT USING FRESH SHRIMP, YOU CAN USE FROZEN SHRIMP. JUST LET THEM DEFROST FOR 10 TO 20 MINUTES BEFORE COOKING THEM.

NUTRITION: 1 SERVING = 8 SHRIMP
CALORIES 188.3 KCAL
CARBOHYDRATE 0.3 G
TOTAL FAT 2.7 G
SATURATED FAT 0.4 G
TRANS FATS 0 G
SODIUM 548.5 MG
TOTAL SUGARS 0 G
PROTEIN 40.8 G
FIBER 0 G

COCONUT CURRY SHRIMP

YIELD: 16 SHRIMP,
2 SERVINGS
PREP TIME: 5 MINUTES
COOK TIME: 5 MINUTES

INGREDIENTS

16 jumbo shrimp, peeled
   and deveined
1 teaspoon (5 ml) avocado oil
½ teaspoon curry powder
¼ teaspoon salt
1 recipe Coconut Curry Peanut
   Sauce (page 135), for serving

INSTRUCTIONS

1. In a large bowl, toss the shrimp with the avocado oil. Add the curry powder and salt and toss to coat.

2. Place the shrimp on the air fryer rack. It's okay if the shrimp are touching as they won't get too crispy. Air-fry them at 400°F (200°C) for 5 minutes.

3. Transfer the shrimp to a large bowl, add the sauce, and toss to coat.

4. Serve the shrimp immediately, or over cauliflower rice, if desired.

TIP: IF YOU'RE NOT SURE ABOUT USING FRESH SHRIMP, YOU CAN USE FROZEN SHRIMP. JUST LET THEM DEFROST FOR 10 TO 20 MINUTES BEFORE COOKING THEM.

NUTRITION: 1 SERVING = 8 SHRIMP
CALORIES 598.5 KCAL
CARBOHYDRATE 9.2 G
TOTAL FAT 40.7 G
SATURATED FAT 26.6 G
TRANS FATS 0 G
SODIUM 1553.3 MG
TOTAL SUGARS 4.8 G
PROTEIN 45.8 G
FIBER 2.1 G

GARLIC BUTTER SHRIMP

YIELD: 16 SHRIMP,
2 SERVINGS
PREP TIME: 5 MINUTES
COOK TIME: 5 MINUTES

INGREDIENTS

16 jumbo shrimp, peeled
and deveined

2 teaspoons (10 g) unsalted butter,
melted, plus more for dipping

¾ teaspoon garlic powder

¼ teaspoon salt

INSTRUCTIONS

1. Place the shrimp in a large bowl. In a small bowl, combine the melted butter, garlic powder, and salt. Pour the mixture over the shrimp and toss to coat.

2. Grease the air fryer rack (or use greased foil or parchment paper if your air fryer cautions against greasing the rack). Place the shrimp on the rack. It's okay if the shrimp are touching as they won't get too crispy.

3. Air-fry at 400°F (200°C) for 5 minutes, or until they are no longer pink on the inside.

4. Serve the shrimp with more melted butter for dipping, if desired.

NUTRITION: 1 SERVING = 8 SHRIMP
CALORIES 206.3 KCAL
CARBOHYDRATE 1.2 G
TOTAL FAT 4.3 G
SATURATED FAT 2.5 G
TRANS FATS 0.2 G
SODIUM 514.7 MG
TOTAL SUGARS 0 G
PROTEIN 41 G
FIBER 0.1 G

COCONUT-CRUSTED SHRIMP

YIELD: 2 SERVINGS OF 8 SHRIMP

PREP TIME: 10 MINUTES

COOK TIME: 6 TO 8 MINUTES

INGREDIENTS

2 tablespoons (16 g) coconut flour

¼ teaspoon garlic powder

¼ teaspoon paprika

¼ cup (20 g) unsweetened coconut flakes

¼ cup (7.5 g) crushed pork rinds

1 large egg

16 jumbo shrimp, peeled and deveined

¼ teaspoon salt

1 recipe Sweet Chili Sauce (page 145), optional

TIP: IF YOU'RE NOT SURE ABOUT USING FRESH SHRIMP, YOU CAN USE FROZEN SHRIMP. JUST LET THEM DEFROST FOR 10 TO 20 MINUTES BEFORE COOKING THEM.

NUTRITION: 1 SERVING = 8 SHRIMP
CALORIES 356.9 KCAL
CARBOHYDRATE 10.3 G
TOTAL FAT 12.8 G
SATURATED FAT 8.3 G
TRANS FATS 0 G
SODIUM 1330.5 MG
TOTAL SUGARS 3.6 G
PROTEIN 49.9 G
FIBER 4.6 G

INSTRUCTIONS

1. Combine the coconut flour, garlic powder, and paprika in a shallow dish or plate and set it aside.

2. Combine the coconut flakes and crushed pork rinds in another shallow dish or plate and set it aside.

3. Beat the egg in a medium-size shallow baking dish and add a splash of water to make an egg wash.

4. Season the shrimp all over with the salt.

5. Dip the shrimp into the coconut flour mixture, then into the egg wash, and then into the coconut flake mixture.

6. Grease the air fryer rack (or use greased foil or parchment paper if your air fryer cautions against greasing the rack). Place the shrimp on the rack, not touching, if possible.

7. Air-fry the shrimp at 375°F (190°C) for 6 to 8 minutes, or until they are golden brown, flipping them halfway through if you are using foil.

8. Serve the shrimp with the sauce.

LEMON DILL SALMON

YIELD: 4 SALMON FILLETS
PREP TIME: 5 MINUTES
COOK TIME: 12 TO
15 MINUTES

INGREDIENTS

1 teaspoon (5 ml) lemon juice

1 teaspoon (5 ml) avocado oil

¼ teaspoon onion powder

¼ teaspoon garlic powder

¼ teaspoon salt

4 (6-ounce [168 g]) salmon filets

1 recipe Lemon Dill Sauce
   (page 143)

INSTRUCTIONS

1. In a small bowl, whisk the lemon juice, avocado oil, onion powder, garlic powder, and salt until fully combined.

2. Brush both sides of the salmon with lemon-spice mixture.

3. Grease the air fryer rack (or use greased foil or parchment paper if your air fryer cautions against greasing the rack). Place the salmon, skin side up, on the rack.

4. Air-fry the salmon at 350°F (180°C) for 12 to 15 minutes, or until the skin is crispy.

5. Remove the salmon carefully from the air fryer with a spatula, trying to make sure it doesn't flake away.

6. Serve the salmon with the sauce.

NUTRITION: 1 SERVING = 1 SALMON FILLET
CALORIES 338.1 KCAL
CARBOHYDRATE 1.7 G
TOTAL FAT 20 G
SATURATED FAT 4.2 G
TRANS FATS 0.2 G
SODIUM 535.6 MG
TOTAL SUGARS 0.7 G
PROTEIN 38.1 G
FIBER 0.2 G

YIELD: 4 SERVINGS,
¼ POUND (113.5 G)
SCALLOPS EACH
PREP TIME: 5 MINUTES
COOK TIME: 6 MINUTES

SPICY SCALLOPS

INGREDIENTS

1 pound (454 g) sea scallops (fresh preferred, but frozen and defrosted will work)

1 tablespoon (15 ml) avocado oil

5 tablespoons (40 g) Cajun Seasoning (page 154)

1 tablespoon (14 g) unsalted butter, melted, for serving (optional)

Lemon wedges, for serving (optional)

INSTRUCTIONS

1. Pat the scallops dry with a paper towel.

2. In a large bowl, combine the avocado oil and Cajun seasoning. Add the scallops and toss to coat.

3. Grease the air fryer rack (or use greased foil or parchment paper if your air fryer cautions against greasing the rack). Place the scallops on the rack, giving them some space if possible.

4. Air-fry the scallops at 400°F (200°C) for 3 minutes. Flip them with tongs or a fork and air-fry them for 3 minutes longer.

5. Serve the scallops with the melted butter and lemon wedges, if desired.

TIP: FOR AN ALTERNATIVE SPICE MIXTURE, COMBINE 1 TEASPOON (6 G) SALT, 1 TEASPOON (2 G) PAPRIKA, 1 TEASPOON (3 G) GARLIC POWDER, ½ TEASPOON ONION POWDER, ½ TEASPOON DRIED PARSLEY, AND ¼ TEASPOON CAYENNE PEPPER.

NUTRITION: 1 SERVING = ¼ RECIPE
CALORIES 105.9 KCAL
CARBOHYDRATE 3.2 G
TOTAL FAT 4 G
SATURATED FAT 0.4 G
TRANS FATS 0 G
SODIUM 740.9 MG
TOTAL SUGARS 0.1 G
PROTEIN 14.3 G
FIBER 0.4 G

FISH CAKES

YIELD: 8 FISH CAKES
PREP TIME: 10 MINUTES
COOK TIME: 6 TO
8 MINUTES

INGREDIENTS

1 (8-ounce [227 g]) can sardines packed in olive oil

1 large egg

2 tablespoons (8 g) minced celery

2 tablespoons (8 g) chopped parsley

1 tablespoon (15 ml) Dijon mustard

½ teaspoon salt

½ teaspoon your favorite keto-friendly hot sauce (e.g., Frank's)

½ cup (15 g) Crumb Coating (page 152)

1 recipe Everything Sauce (page 138), for serving

Lemon wedges, for serving

NUTRITION: 1 SERVING = 1 FISH CAKE
CALORIES 95 KCAL
CARBOHYDRATE 1.8 G
TOTAL FAT 7.4 G
SATURATED FAT 2.1 G
TRANS FATS 0.1 G
SODIUM 365.7 MG
TOTAL SUGARS 0.7 G
PROTEIN 5.2 G
FIBER 0.3 G

INSTRUCTIONS

1. Drain the oil from the sardines and lay them out on a cutting board. Chop them roughly and transfer them to a medium-size bowl.

2. Beat the egg in a small bowl, and then add that to the bowl of sardines.

3. Add the celery, parsley, mustard, salt, and hot sauce to the bowl. With a wooden spoon or clean hands, combine the ingredients into a sticky dough.

4. Spread the crumb coating in a shallow dish.

5. Grease the air fryer rack (or use greased foil or parchment paper if your air fryer cautions against greasing the rack).

6. Divide the fish cake mixture into 8 portions and roll each into a ball. Roll each fish cake in the crumb coating and place it on the air fryer rack. It's okay if they're close and touching, but they should not be stacked.

7. Air-fry the fish cakes at 375°F (190°C) for 6 to 8 minutes, or until the crumb coating is crisp.

8. Serve the fish cakes with the sauce and lemon wedges.

STAR INGREDIENT
VEGETABLES

BALSAMIC MUSHROOMS

YIELD: **4 SERVINGS**
PREP TIME: **6 MINUTES**
COOK TIME: **8 MINUTES**

INGREDIENTS

8 ounces (224 g) baby
bella mushrooms

4 tablespoons (56 g) unsalted
butter, melted, divided

2 tablespoons (30 ml) avocado oil

1 teaspoon (6 g) salt

1 tablespoon (15 ml) balsamic vinegar

1 teaspoon (5 ml) coconut aminos
or tamari

½ teaspoon garlic powder

INSTRUCTIONS

1. Rinse or pat the mushrooms clean. Trim the ends of the mushroom stems to remove any dry bits. Cut the mushrooms in half or quarters. Aim for large bite-size pieces, as the mushrooms will shrink when cooked.

2. Transfer the mushrooms to a bowl, add 2 tablespoons (15 ml) of the melted butter, the avocado oil, and the salt. Toss to coat.

3. Line the air fryer tray with parchment paper and spread the mushrooms in a single layer. Air-fry the mushrooms at 350°F (180°C) for 6 minutes.

4. While the mushrooms are cooking, combine the remaining 2 tablespoons (15 ml) melted butter, the balsamic vinegar, the coconut aminos, and the garlic powder in the same bowl.

5. Add the cooked mushrooms to the sauce and toss to coat.

NUTRITION: 1 SERVING
CALORIES 187 KCAL
CARBOHYDRATE 3.6 G
TOTAL FAT 18.3 G
SATURATED FAT 7.9 G
TRANS FATS 0 G
SODIUM 621 MG
TOTAL SUGARS 1.52 G
PROTEIN 2.1 G
FIBER 1.3 G

BUFFALO MUSHROOMS

YIELD: 4 SERVINGS
PREP TIME: 5 MINUTES
COOK TIME: 6 MINUTES

INGREDIENTS

1 pound (454 g) whole button mushrooms
1 teaspoon (5 ml) avocado oil
1 recipe Crumb Coating (page 152)
½ teaspoon salt
1 recipe Buffalo Sauce (page 134)

INSTRUCTIONS

1. Rinse or pat the mushrooms clean. Trim the ends of the mushroom stems to remove any dry bits. Place the mushrooms in a medium-size bowl.

2. Add the avocado oil and toss to coat. Add the crumb coating and toss to cover the mushrooms completely.

3. Grease the air fryer rack (or use greased foil or parchment paper if your air fryer cautions against greasing the rack). Spread the mushrooms on the greased rack (it's okay if they're touching).

4. Air-fry the mushrooms at 400°F (200°C) for 7 minutes, or until the crumb coating is browned.

5. Remove the mushrooms carefully (they'll have probably released some moisture) and sprinkle them with the salt.

6. When the mushrooms are done, either toss them with the sauce in a bowl or serve the sauce on the side for dipping.

NUTRITION: 1 SERVING
CALORIES 210 KCAL
CARBOHYDRATE 4.1 G
TOTAL FAT 16.3 G
SATURATED FAT 7.1 G
TRANS FATS 0 G
SODIUM 1310 MG
TOTAL SUGARS 2 G
PROTEIN 14.4 G
FIBER 1.2 G

BUFFALO CAULIFLOWER

YIELD: 2 SERVINGS
PREP TIME: 5 MINUTES
COOK TIME: 6 MINUTES

INGREDIENTS

- 1 large egg
- 1 recipe Crumb Coating (page 152)
- 1 pound (454 g) frozen cauliflower florets, defrosted
- 1 recipe Buffalo Sauce (page 134)

INSTRUCTIONS

1. Beat the egg in a medium-size shallow baking dish and add a splash of water to make an egg wash.

2. Place the crumb coating in a second shallow dish.

3. Dip each cauliflower floret into the egg wash and then into the crumb coating, covering completely and pressing firmly to adhere.

4. Grease the air fryer rack (or use greased foil or parchment paper if your air fryer cautions against greasing the rack). Spread the florets in a single layer.

5. Air-fry the cauliflower at 400°F (200°C) for 8 to 10 minutes, or until crispy.

6. When the cauliflower is done, either toss it with the sauce in a bowl or serve the sauce on the side for dipping.

NUTRITION: 1 SERVING
CALORIES 406 KCAL
CARBOHYDRATE 13.8 G
TOTAL FAT 26.9 G
SATURATED FAT 13 G
TRANS FATS 0 G
SODIUM 2740 MG
TOTAL SUGARS 5.4 G
PROTEIN 29.7 G
FIBER 5.4 G

BUTTERY KABOCHA SQUASH

YIELD: 4 SERVINGS
PREP TIME: 5 MINUTES
COOK TIME: 6 MINUTES

INGREDIENTS

1 medium kabocha squash

2 teaspoons (12 g) salt

½ teaspoon ground cinnamon

¼ teaspoon ground nutmeg

4 tablespoons (56 g) unsalted butter, melted

TIP: USE THE CONVECTION/BAKE SETTING IF YOUR AIR FRYER HAS IT. THIS WILL PROVIDE A CRISPIER BOTTOM.

NUTRITION: 1 SERVING
CALORIES 203 KCAL
CARBOHYDRATE 23.7 G
TOTAL FAT 11.5 G
SATURATED FAT 7.2 G
TRANS FATS 0 G
SODIUM 1180 MG
TOTAL SUGARS 10.03 G
PROTEIN 3.4 G
FIBER 3.5 G

INSTRUCTIONS

1. Cut the squash in half through the stem. Use a spoon to scrape the inside of the squash and remove the seeds and strings. Place each half flesh-side down and cut it into 1-inch (2.5 cm) strips. This should make crescent-like fries.

2. In a large bowl, combine the salt, cinnamon, and nutmeg and stir. Add the squash slices and melted butter and toss to coat thoroughly.

3. Place a silicone mat or parchment paper on the lower rack. Spread the squash pieces on the tray (it's okay if they're touching).

4. Air-fry the squash at 350°F (180°C) for 10 to 15 minutes, or until golden brown, flipping the slices halfway through so they brown evenly.

CAULIFLOWER MAC 'N CHEESE

YIELD: 4 SERVINGS
PREP TIME: 16 MINUTES
COOK TIME: 10 MINUTES

INGREDIENTS

1 pound (454 g) cauliflower florets, fresh or frozen and defrosted

½ cup (120 ml) heavy cream

½ cup (120 ml) chicken broth

1 (8-ounce [227 g]) package cream cheese

2½ cups (260 g) shredded cheddar cheese, divided

½ teaspoon garlic powder

¼ teaspoon chili powder

1 teaspoon (6 g) salt

¼ cup (7.5 g) crushed pork rinds

4 slices bacon, diced and cooked to desired crispiness

INSTRUCTIONS

1. If you are using fresh cauliflower, steam the florets until they are tender, about 5 minutes. Drain them and allow them to come to room temperature before making the mac and cheese.

2. Pour the cream and broth into a large saucepan and heat over medium-low heat until it begins to simmer.

3. Add the cream , 2 cups (210 g) of the shredded cheese, the garlic powder, the chili powder, and the salt to the saucepan and whisk to combine and melt the cheese, about 5 minutes.

4. Once the sauce is smooth, fold in the cauliflower until it is coated. Transfer it to a ceramic baking dish or cast-iron dish that fits in your air fryer. Sprinkle the cauliflower with the remaining ½ cup (52 g) shredded cheese, the pork rinds, and the bacon.

5. Air-fry the cauliflower at 450°F (230°C) for 4 to 6 minutes, or until it is golden brown.

6. Remove the cauliflower carefully with oven mitts as the dish will be very hot. Allow it to cool for 5 minutes.

NUTRITION: 1 SERVING
CALORIES 662 KCAL
CARBOHYDRATE 12.3 G
TOTAL FAT 57.2 G
SATURATED FAT 32.8 G
TRANS FATS 1.8 G
SODIUM 1548 MG
TOTAL SUGARS 6.2 G
PROTEIN 27.3 G
FIBER 2.7 G

13.8 G NET CARBS = 25.3 G CARBOHYDRATES - 11.5 G FIBER

CAJUN CAULIFLOWER STEAK

YIELD: 4 SERVINGS
PREP TIME: 5 MINUTES
COOK TIME: 6 MINUTES

INGREDIENTS

1 large head cauliflower

¼ teaspoon garlic powder

½ teaspoon Cajun Seasoning (page 154)

¼ teaspoon salt

½ cup (112 g) unsalted butter, melted

1 recipe Chimichurri (page 136), for serving (optional)

INSTRUCTIONS

1. Wash the cauliflower and cut off any green leaves at the stem. Cut the cauliflower into 1-inch (2.5 cm) slices to make thick vegetable steaks. The steaks you cut in the middle will be much heartier than the ones on the sides.

2. In a small bowl, combine the garlic powder, Cajun seasoning, and salt. Add the melted butter and stir to combine.

3. Place the cauliflower steaks on the rack and brush liberally with the seasoned butter.

4. Air-fry the cauliflower at 350°F (180°C) for 10 minutes. Flip the steaks over and brush them liberally with the seasoned butter. Air-fry them for 8 minutes longer.

5. Remove the cauliflower carefully with a spatula or tongs. The florets at the top may be light and floppy. Serve the cauliflower with the chimichurri, if desired.

NUTRITION: 1 SERVING
CALORIES 422 KCAL
CARBOHYDRATE 13.1 G
TOTAL FAT 41.6 G
SATURATED FAT 16.5 G
TRANS FATS 1 G
SODIUM 236 MG
TOTAL SUGARS 4.1 G
PROTEIN 4 G
FIBER 5.4 G

CHEDDAR AND CHIVE CAULI TOTS

YIELD: 12 TOTS,
2 SERVINGS
PREP TIME: 17 MINUTES
COOK TIME: 10 MINUTES

INGREDIENTS

12 ounces (340 g) cooked cauliflower rice or frozen cauliflower rice, defrosted

½ cup (24 g) chopped fresh chives or 3 tablespoons (1 g) freeze-dried chives

2 tablespoons (10 g) grated Parmesan cheese

1½ ounces (42 g) ground pork rinds

3 ounces (84 g) sharp cheddar cheese, shredded

2 large eggs, beaten

2 teaspoons (12 g) salt

1 teaspoon (2 g) onion powder

1 teaspoon (3 g) garlic powder

1 recipe your favorite sauce (pages 132 to 151), for serving

INSTRUCTIONS

1. Place the cauliflower rice in the center of a clean dish towel and squeeze to remove any excess liquid.

2. Stir the cauliflower rice, chives, Parmesan cheese, pork rinds, shredded cheddar, eggs, salt, onion powder, and garlic powder to combine in a bowl.

3. Divide the mixture into 12 even portions and roll them into balls.

4. Grease the air fryer rack (or use greased foil or parchment paper if your air fryer cautions against greasing the rack). Place the cauli tots in the air fryer basket. It's okay if they're touching, but if they're further apart they'll be crispier. They should not be layered.

5. Air-fry the cauli tots at 400°F (200°C) for 10 minutes.

6. Remove the cauli tots with a spatula and let them cool on some parchment paper.

7. Enjoy the cauli tots immediately by dipping them in your favorite sauce, or store them in an airtight container for easy snacking during the week.

NUTRITION: 1 SERVING = 6 TOTS
CALORIES 442 KCAL   (WITH CHIMICHURRI SAUCE)
CARBOHYDRATE 18.4 G
TOTAL FAT 34.1 G
SATURATED FAT 9.3 G
TRANS FATS 0 G
SODIUM 1756 MG
TOTAL SUGARS 5.9 G
PROTEIN 20.8 G
FIBER 5.7 G

12.6 G NET CARBS = 21.2 G CARBOHYDRATES - 8.6 G FIBER

CRISPY BRUSSELS SPROUTS

YIELD: 2 SERVINGS
PREP TIME: 25 MINUTES
COOK TIME: 10 MINUTES

INGREDIENTS

1 pound (454 g) whole Brussels sprouts

¼ cup (20 g) raw chopped bacon

1 teaspoon (6 g) salt

½ teaspoon garlic powder

1 teaspoon (5 ml) apple cider vinegar

TIP: THESE CAN BE COOKED DIRECTLY IN THE BASKET, BUT THEY TASTE ESPECIALLY GOOD WHEN COOKED IN A CAST-IRON PAN SMALL ENOUGH FOR THE AIR FRYER. YOU CAN REPLACE THE BACON WITH PANCETTA IF YOU WANT TO MAKE THESE A LITTLE BIT FANCIER.

NUTRITION: 1 SERVING
CALORIES 148 KCAL
CARBOHYDRATE 21.1 G
TOTAL FAT 4.2 G
SATURATED FAT 1.3 G
TRANS FATS 0 G
SODIUM 1404 MG
TOTAL SUGARS 5.1 G
PROTEIN 11.2 G
FIBER 8.7 G

INSTRUCTIONS

1. Bring a large pot of salted water to a boil over high heat.

2. Add the Brussels sprouts and blanch them until they are bright green, 3 to 5 minutes. Drain.

3. Lightly sauté the bacon in a skillet over medium-low heat. Each side should cook for no more than 3 minutes. Keeping the fat in the pan, remove the bacon before the desired crispiness is reached because the grease on the bacon will continue cooking it and make it crispier once it's out of the pan.

4. Slice the Brussels sprouts in half through the stem and toss them in the pan with the bacon fat. Add the salt and garlic powder and stir to coat.

5. Transfer the Brussels sprouts to a cast-iron pan that fits in your air fryer and add the cooked bacon.

6. Air-fry the Brussels sprouts at 400°F (200°C) for 7 to 10 minutes, or until they reach the desired crispiness.

7. Sprinkle the Brussels sprouts with the apple cider vinegar and serve.

GARLIC PARMESAN ASPARAGUS

YIELD: 2 SERVINGS
PREP TIME: 25 MINUTES
COOK TIME: 10 MINUTES

INGREDIENTS

1 bundle asparagus

1 tablespoon (15 ml) avocado oil

2 teaspoons (6 g) garlic powder

1 teaspoon (6 g) salt

1 teaspoon (2 g) red pepper flakes (optional)

⅓ cup (28 g) grated Parmesan cheese

INSTRUCTIONS

1. Trim off the woody ends of the asparagus spears and rinse them. Pat them dry with paper towels.

2. On a large plate or baking dish, lay out the asparagus spears and coat them thoroughly with the avocado oil.

3. Add the garlic powder, salt, and red pepper flakes (if using). Make sure the spices are evenly distributed.

4. Grease the air fryer rack (or use greased foil or parchment paper if your air fryer cautions against greasing the rack).

5. Lay the spears in the air fryer basket so the asparagus is touching but not overlapping. Sprinkle them with the Parmesan.

6. Air-fry the asparagus at 375°F (190°C) for 8 to 10 minutes, or until the cheese and the asparagus spears are golden brown.

NUTRITION: 1 SERVING
CALORIES 154 KCAL
CARBOHYDRATE 6.3 G
TOTAL FAT 11.9 G
SATURATED FAT 3.4 G
TRANS FATS 0 G
SODIUM 1482 MG
TOTAL SUGARS 0.8 G
PROTEIN 6.4 G
FIBER 1.1 G

GARLIC PARMESAN GREEN BEANS

YIELD: 2 SERVINGS
PREP TIME: 12 MINUTES
COOK TIME: 8 MINUTES

INGREDIENTS

1 pound (454 g) fresh green beans

1 large egg

½ recipe Crumb Coating (page 152)

1 teaspoon (6 g) salt

1 teaspoon (3 g) garlic powder

1 recipe your favorite sauce (pages 132 to 151), for serving (optional)

INSTRUCTIONS

1. Beat the egg in a medium-size shallow baking dish and add a splash of water to make an egg wash.

2. Place the crumb coating in a second shallow dish

3. In small bunches, add the green beans to the egg wash, and then roll them in the crumb coating, covering completely and pressing firmly to adhere. Sprinkle with the salt and garlic powder.

4. Grease the air fryer rack (or use greased foil or parchment paper if your air fryer cautions against greasing the rack). Place the beans in the air fryer basket (it's okay if they touch).

5. Air-fry the beans at 400°F (200°C) for 8 minutes, or until the crumb coating is crispy, tossing a bit halfway through so that all sides get crispy.

6. Serve the beans as is or with your favorite sauce.

NUTRITION: 1 SERVING
CALORIES 243 KCAL
CARBOHYDRATE 21.4 G
TOTAL FAT 10.4 G
SATURATED FAT 3.6 G
TRANS FATS 0 G
SODIUM 2352 MG
TOTAL SUGARS 9.8 G
PROTEIN 18 G
FIBER 3.4 G

SPAGHETTI SQUASH

YIELD: 4 SERVINGS
PREP TIME: 7 MINUTES
COOK TIME: 25 MINUTES

INGREDIENTS

1 (3- to 4-pound [1.4 to 1.8 kg]) spaghetti squash
2 teaspoons (10 ml) avocado oil
1 teaspoon (6 g) salt
⅛ teaspoon ground nutmeg
⅛ teaspoon ground cinnamon

INSTRUCTIONS

1. Carefully cut the squash in half lengthwise. Depending on the size of your air fryer, you might want to cut it into medallions so that they fit evenly.

2. Remove the seeds and strands. If you cut the squash lengthwise, scrape it out with a spoon; if you cut it into medallions, use a paring knife to cut out the seeds at the center.

3. Brush the flesh side of the spaghetti squash with the avocado oil.

4. Place the squash on the air fryer rack flesh-side up and air-fry them it at 350°F (180°C) for about 25 minutes, until you can easily pierce the squash with a fork. (The time may vary depending on the size of your squash.)

5. Remove the squash and use a fork to scrape the flesh into "noodles." Transfer to a large bowl.

6. Add the salt, nutmeg, and cinnamon and toss to coat.

TIP: YOU CAN SERVE THIS WITH ANY OF THE SAUCES (PAGES 132 TO 151) OR WITH SUGAR-FREE MARINARA FOR A MORE SAVORY SPAGHETTI SQUASH EXPERIENCE.

NUTRITION: 1 SERVING
CALORIES 123 KCAL
CARBOHYDRATE 12.6 G
TOTAL FAT 8.5 G
SATURATED FAT 3.9 G
TRANS FATS 0 G
SODIUM 625 MG
TOTAL SUGARS 4.9 G
PROTEIN 1.3 G
FIBER 2.7 G

VEGGIE KEBABS

YIELD: 2 SERVINGS
PREP TIME: 11 MINUTES
COOK TIME: 10 MINUTES

INGREDIENTS

1 pound (454 g) button mushrooms

2 bell peppers, any color

2 zucchinis

½ red onion

½ cup (120 ml) Greek Dressing and Marinade (page 141)

1 teaspoon (6 g) salt

INSTRUCTIONS

1. Trim the ends of the mushroom stems to remove any dry bits. Cut the peppers, zucchinis, and onion into large bite-size pieces. Transfer all the vegetables into a large bowl.

2. Add the marinade and toss the vegetables until fully coated.

3. Refrigerate the vegetables for at least 1 hour. If your are using wooden skewers, soak them in water while the vegetables are marinating.

4. Assemble the skewers by alternating vegetables along their lengths. Place them on the air fryer rack and sprinkle with the salt.

5. Air-fry the kebabs at 400°F (200°C) for 8 to 10 minutes, until they are tender and lightly brown.

NUTRITION: 1 SERVING
CALORIES 662 KCAL
CARBOHYDRATE 28 G
TOTAL FAT 56.9 G
SATURATED FAT 6.7 G
TRANS FATS 0 G
SODIUM 2470 MG
TOTAL SUGARS 16.9 G
PROTEIN 13.6 G
FIBER 10.8 G

DESSERTS

BLACKBERRY HAND PIES

YIELD: 4 HAND PIES
PREP TIME: 20 MINUTES
COOK TIME: 26 MINUTES

INGREDIENTS

1 cup (150 g) blackberries, fresh or frozen

2 tablespoons (24 g) brown granulated sweetener (I prefer erythritol)

1 tablespoon (15 ml) lemon juice

Pinch of salt

1 recipe Sweet Protein Dough (page 130)

TIP: FOR HAND PIE RECIPES, USE THE CONVECTION/BAKE SETTING IF YOUR AIR FRYER HAS IT. THIS WILL MEAN YOU DON'T NEED TO FLIP THE HAND PIES MID-BAKE.

NUTRITION: 1 SERVING = 1 HAND PIE
CALORIES 323.2 KCAL
CARBOHYDRATE 8.7 G
TOTAL FAT 23.4 G
SATURATED FAT 9.6 G
TRANS FATS 0.5 G
SODIUM 747.9 MG
TOTAL SUGARS 3.2 G
PROTEIN 20.8 G
FIBER 3.2 G

INSTRUCTIONS

1. Simmer the blackberries, sweetener, lemon juice, and salt into a saucepan over medium heat, breaking apart the berries with a wooden spoon, until it is thickened to a sticky compote consistency, about 15 minutes. Remove it from the heat.

2. Divide the dough into 4 equal portions and place them on a piece of parchment paper. Cover them with another piece of parchment. Use a rolling pin to roll out each to a ½-inch (1.3 cm) thick round.

3. Add 2 tablespoons (30 g) of the filling to one side and fold it over, pressing the edges with a fork to crimp and seal. Repeat it for the remaining hand pies.

4. Line the air fryer rack with parchment paper or greased foil and place the hand pies in a single layer.

5. Air-fry the hand pies at 350°F (180°C) for 6 minutes, or until the top is golden brown.

6. Flip the hand pies and remove the parchment paper. Air-fry the hand pies for an additional 5 minutes, or until they are golden brown.

7. Remove the hand pies from the air fryer and allow them to rest for 5 minutes. Store in an airtight container for up to a week.

CHEESECAKE HAND PIES

YIELD: 4 HAND PIES
PREP TIME: 20 MINUTES
COOK TIME: 11 MINUTES

INGREDIENTS

½ cup (120 ml) heavy cream, cold

½ cup (120 g) cream cheese, softened

¼ cup (30 g) powdered sweetener

1   teaspoon (5 ml) lemon juice

¼ teaspoon vanilla extract

1   recipe Sweet Protein Dough (page 130)

INSTRUCTIONS

1. In a stand mixer or in a bowl with a hand mixer, whip the heavy cream on low speed and slowly increase the speed to medium until it forms stiff peaks.

2. In a separate bowl, whisk the cream cheese, sweetener, lemon juice, and vanilla .

3. Gently fold the cream cheese mixture into the whipped cream and whip until combined.

4. Divide the dough into 4 equal portions and place them between two sheets of parchment paper. Use a rolling pin to roll out each to a ½-inch (1.3 cm) thick round.

5. Add 2 tablespoons (30 g) of the filling to one side and fold over, crimping and sealing the edges with a fork. Repeat for the remaining hand pies.

6. Line the air fryer rack with parchment paper or greased foil. Place the hand pies in a single layer.

7. Air-fry the hand pies at 350°F (180°C) for 6 minutes, or until the top is golden brown.

8. Flip the hand pies and remove the parchment paper. Air-fry them for an additional 5 minutes, or until they are golden brown.

9. Remove the hand pies from the air fryer and allow them to cool before serving.

NUTRITION: 1 SERVING = 1 HAND PIE
CALORIES 504.1 KCAL
CARBOHYDRATE 7.7 G
TOTAL FAT 43.2 G
SATURATED FAT 21.9 G
TRANS FATS 1.1 G
SODIUM 844.2 MG
TOTAL SUGARS 3.3 G
PROTEIN 22.9 G
FIBER 1.3 G

MOCK APPLE HAND PIES

YIELD: 4 HAND PIES

PREP TIME: 20 MINUTES

COOK TIME: 35 MINUTES

INGREDIENTS

2 tablespoons (28 g) unsalted butter

2 tablespoons (24 g) brown granulated sweetener (I prefer erythritol)

1 teaspoon (3 g) ground cinnamon

½ teaspoon ground nutmeg

⅛ teaspoon ground cloves

1 cup (130 g) diced jicama

1 tablespoon (15 ml) water

1 tablespoon (15 ml) lemon juice

1 teaspoon (5 ml) vanilla extract

Pinch of salt

1 recipe Sweet Protein Dough (page 130)

1 large egg (optional)

NUTRITION: 1 SERVING = 1 HAND PIE
CALORIES 368.6 KCAL
CARBOHYDRATE 6.9 G
TOTAL FAT 29.1 G
SATURATED FAT 13.3 G
TRANS FATS 0.7 G
SODIUM 787.8 MG
TOTAL SUGARS 1.7 G
PROTEIN 20.5 G
FIBER 2.1 G

INSTRUCTIONS

1. Melt the butter in a saucepan over medium heat. Add the sweetener, cinnamon, nutmeg, and cloves. Stir to combine and dissolve the sweetener.

2. Add the jicama, water, lemon juice, vanilla, and salt and let the mixture simmer for 20 minutes, or until the jicama is softened. Remove it from the heat.

3. Divide the dough into 4 equal portions and place them on a piece of parchment paper. Cover them with another piece of parchment. Use a rolling pin to roll each out to a ½-inch (1.3 cm) thick round.

4. Add 2 tablespoons (30 g) of the filling to one side of a round and fold the other side over, pressing the edges with a fork to crimp and seal. Repeat for the remaining hand pies.

5. Line the air fryer rack with parchment paper or greased foil and place the hand pies in a single layer. Brush with egg wash if desired.

6. Air-fry the hand pies at 350°F (180°C) for 6 minutes, or until the top is golden brown.

7. Flip the hand pies and remove the parchment paper. Air-fry the hand pies for an additional 5 minutes, or until golden brown.

8. Remove the hand pies from the air fryer and allow them to rest for 5 minutes. Store them in an airtight container for up to a week.

CARROT CAKE MUFFINS

YIELD: 12 MUFFINS

PREP TIME: 15 MINUTES

COOK TIME: 20 MINUTES

INGREDIENTS

- 2 cups (180 g) shredded carrots
- 2 cups (240 g) almond flour
- 1 cup (200 g) granulated sugar substitute (e.g., Swerve)
- 2 tablespoons (16 g) coconut flour
- 2 teaspoons (10 g) baking soda
- ½ teaspoon baking powder
- 1 tablespoon (7 g) ground nutmeg
- 2 tablespoons and 1 teaspoon (18 g) ground cinnamon
- ½ teaspoon ginger powder
- ½ teaspoon salt
- 4 large eggs
- ⅓ cup (80 ml) avocado oil
- 1 tablespoon (15 ml) vanilla extract
- 4 tablespoons (56 g) unsalted butter, melted
- 1 cup (140 g) coarsely chopped walnuts (optional)

Silicone muffin liners

NUTRITION: 1 SERVING = 1 MUFFIN
CALORIES 246.7 KCAL
CARBOHYDRATE 8.8 G
TOTAL FAT 21.5 G
SATURATED FAT 4.7 G
TRANS FATS 0.2 G
SODIUM 372.2 MG
TOTAL SUGARS 2.5 G
PROTEIN 6.5 G
FIBER 4.2 G

INSTRUCTIONS

1. In the bowl of a food processor, pulse the shredded carrots, almond flour, sugar substitute, coconut flour, baking soda, baking powder, nutmeg, cinnamon, ginger powder, and salt to combine.

2. In a small bowl, combine the eggs, avocado oil, and vanilla. Add the mixture to the food processor and pulse to combine.

3. Melt the butter, add it to food processor, and pulse to combine.

4. Add the walnuts, if using, and pulse to combine.

5. Grease 12 silicone muffin liners. Divide the batter among the muffin liners so that they are no more than three-fourths full. Depending on the size of your air fryer, you may need to cook the muffins in batches.

6. Air-fry the muffins at 300°F (150°C) for 20 minutes. They are done when you can insert a toothpick and remove it clean.

7. Remove the muffins from the air fryer and allow them to cool for 5 minutes. Store them in an airtight container in the fridge for up to a week.

TIP: USE THE CONVECTION/BAKE SETTING IF YOUR AIR FRYER HAS IT FOR A CRISPIER BOTTOM. YOU CAN ALSO REPLACE 1 CUP (120 G) ALMOND FLOUR WITH 1 CUP (30 G) GROUND PORK RINDS FOR A MORE SAVORY MUFFIN.

CHOCOLATE ZUCCHINI MUFFINS

YIELD: 12 MUFFINS
PREP TIME: 15 MINUTES
COOK TIME: 20 MINUTES

INGREDIENTS

2 cups (240 g) grated zucchini (do not remove excess water)

2 cups (240 g) almond flour

1 cup (200 g) granulated sweetener (I prefer erythritol)

½ cup (45 g) cocoa powder

2 tablespoons (16 g) coconut flour

2 teaspoons (10 g) baking soda

½ teaspoon baking powder

½ teaspoon salt

½ teaspoon espresso powder (optional)

4 large eggs

4 tablespoons (56 g) unsalted butter, melted

⅓ cup (80 ml) avocado oil

1 tablespoon (15 ml) vanilla extract

½ cup (75 g) sugar-free chocolate chips (optional, e.g., Lily's)

Silicone muffin liners

NUTRITION: 1 SERVING = 1 MUFFIN
CALORIES 240.9 KCAL
CARBOHYDRATE 7.5 G
TOTAL FAT 21.8 G
SATURATED FAT 4.8 G
TRANS FATS 0.2 G
SODIUM 356.8 MG
TOTAL SUGARS 1.9 G
PROTEIN 7.2 G
FIBER 4 G

INSTRUCTIONS

1. In the bowl of a food processor, pulse the zucchini, almond flour, sweetener, cocoa powder, coconut flour, baking soda, baking powder, salt, and espresso powder (if using) to combine.

2. In a small bowl, combine the eggs, melted butter, avocado oil, and vanilla. Add the mixture to the food processor and pulse to combine.

3. Remove the batter from the food processor and return it to one of the previously used bowls. Stir in the chocolate chips (if using) by hand.

4. Grease 12 silicone muffin liners. Divide the batter among the muffin liners so that they are no more than three-fourths full. Depending on the size of your air fryer, you may need to cook the muffins in batches.

5. Air-fry the muffins at 300°F (150°C) for 20 minutes. They are done when you can insert a toothpick and remove it clean.

6. Remove the muffins from the air fryer and allow them to cool for 5 minutes. Store them in an airtight container in the fridge for up to a week.

ZUCCHINI MUFFINS

YIELD: 12 MUFFINS
PREP TIME: 20 MINUTES
COOK TIME: 20 MINUTES

INGREDIENTS

2 cups (240 g) grated zucchini

½ teaspoon salt, plus more for the zucchini

2 cups (240 g) almond flour

1 cup (200 g) granulated sweetener (I prefer erythritol)

2 tablespoons (16 g) coconut flour

2 teaspoons (10 g) baking soda

½ teaspoon baking powder

1 tablespoon (7 g) ground nutmeg

2 tablespoons and 1 teaspoon (18 g) ground cinnamon

½ teaspoon ginger powder

4 eggs

4 tablespoons (56 g) unsalted butter, melted

⅓ cup (80 ml) avocado oil

1 tablespoon (15 ml) vanilla extract

1 cup (140 g) coarsely chopped walnuts

Silicone muffin liners

NUTRITION: 1 SERVING = 1 MUFFIN
CALORIES 239.7 KCAL
CARBOHYDRATE 7 G
TOTAL FAT 21.5 G
SATURATED FAT 4.7 G
TRANS FATS 0.2 G
SODIUM 356.4 MG
TOTAL SUGARS 1.9 G
PROTEIN 6.6 G
FIBER 3.6 G

INSTRUCTIONS

1. Place the zucchini in a colander and lightly salt it. Set the colander over the sink to drain for 5 minutes. Press as much water out of the zucchini as possible. If your colander's holes are too broad, place the zucchini in a clean dish towel and squeeze the excess moisture out.

2. In the bowl of a food processor, pulse the almond flour, sweetener, coconut flour, baking soda, baking powder, nutmeg, cinnamon, ginger, and salt to combine.

3. In a small bowl, combine the eggs, avocado oil, and vanilla. Add the egg mixture, butter, and zucchini to the food processor and pulse to combine. Add the walnuts, if using, and pulse to combine.

4. Grease 12 silicone muffin liners. Divide the batter among the muffin liners so that they are no more than three-fourths full. You may need to cook the muffins in batches.

5. Air-fry the muffins at 300°F (150°C) for 20 minutes. They are done when you can insert a toothpick and remove it clean.

6. Remove the muffins from the air fryer and allow them to cool for 5 minutes. Store them in an airtight container in the fridge for up to a week.

DOUGHS

PROTEIN CRACKERS

YIELD: 4 SERVINGS
PREP TIME: 15 MINUTES
COOK TIME: 12 MINUTES

INGREDIENTS

2 ounces (56 g) crushed pork rinds

¼ cup (30 g) coconut flour

2 teaspoons (10 g) baking powder

1 tablespoon (3.6 g)
Italian seasoning

½ teaspoon xanthan gum

6 ounces (170 g)
shredded mozzarella

4 tablespoons (57 g) unsalted
butter, softened

3 eggs

1 teaspoon (6 g) flaky sea salt

TIP: USE THE CONVECTION/BAKE SETTING IF YOUR AIR FRYER HAS IT. YOU WON'T NEED TO FLIP THE CRACKERS.

NUTRITION: 1 SERVING = ¼ RECIPE
CALORIES 399.8 KCAL
CARBOHYDRATE 8.1 G
TOTAL FAT 30 G
SATURATED FAT 15.7 G
TRANS FATS 0.8 G
SODIUM 1373.6 MG
TOTAL SUGARS 1.8 G
PROTEIN 25 G
FIBER 3.1 G

INSTRUCTIONS

1. Combine the crushed pork rinds, coconut flour, baking powder, Italian seasoning, and xanthan gum in a food processor.

2. Microwave the mozzarella and butter for 10 seconds at a time, stirring in between to combine until the butter is liquid and the mozzarella is stringy.

3. Add the melted mozzarella mixture and the eggs to the food processor and pulse.

4. Remove the dough from the food processor and gently knead it into a ball until it holds its shape.

5. Place the dough ball between pieces of parchment paper and roll it out very thin. Score with a knife into squares. Sprinkle with salt.

6. Transfer the parchment paper and crackers to the air fryer tray. Cooking time varies based upon thinness. For a 1 mm-thick cracker, air-fry at 300°F (150°C) for 7 minutes. Flip the crackers with a spatula and cook them for an additional 3 minutes. Check to make sure the edges aren't burning.

7. Remove the crackers from the air fryer and allow them to cool to room temperature before eating. Store them in an airtight container in the fridge, where they will keep for 7 to 10 days.

SAVORY PROTEIN DOUGH

YIELD: 4 SERVINGS
PREP TIME: 15 MINUTES
COOK TIME: 2 MINUTES

INGREDIENTS

2 ounces (56 g) crushed pork rinds

3 tablespoons (24 g) coconut flour
or ⅓ cup (40 g) almond flour

1 teaspoon (5 g) baking powder

½ teaspoon garlic powder

½ teaspoon xanthan gum

¼ teaspoon salt

1½ cups (180 g) shredded mozzarella

2 tablespoons (28 g)
unsalted butter

1 large egg

INSTRUCTIONS

1. Pulse the crushed pork rinds, coconut flour, baking powder, garlic powder, xanthan gum, and salt in a food processor to combine and further crush the pork rinds.

2. In a microwave-safe bowl, combine the mozzarella and butter and heat for 10 seconds at a time. Stir in between to combine. The butter should be liquid and the mozzarella should be stringy.

3. Add the egg to the food processor and pulse to combine.

4. Add the melted mozzarella mixture to the food processor and pulse to combine.

5. Remove the dough from the food processor and gently knead it into a ball. When the dough holds its shape, it is ready to be used according to recipe directions.

NUTRITION: 1 SERVING = ¼ RECIPE
CALORIES 306 KCAL
CARBOHYDRATE 5.4 G
TOTAL FAT 23.2 G
SATURATED FAT 9.6 G
TRANS FATS 0.5 G
SODIUM 747.7 MG
TOTAL SUGARS 1.3 G
PROTEIN 20.4 G
FIBER 1.3 G

SWEET PROTEIN DOUGH

YIELD: 4 SERVINGS
PREP TIME: 15 MINUTES
COOK TIME: 2 MINUTES

INGREDIENTS

2 ounces (56 g) crushed pork rinds

3 tablespoons (24 g) coconut flour or ⅓ cup (40 g) almond flour

1 teaspoon (5 g) baking powder

½ teaspoon xanthan gum

¼ teaspoon salt

1½ cups (180 g) shredded mozzarella

2 tablespoons (28 g) unsalted butter

1 large egg

1 teaspoon (5 ml) vanilla extract

¾ cup (90 g) powdered sweetener

INSTRUCTIONS

1. Pulse the crushed pork rinds, coconut flour, baking powder, xanthan gum, and salt in food processor to combine and further crush the pork rinds.

2. In a microwave-safe bowl, heat the mozzarella and butter for 10 seconds at a time. Stir in between to combine. The butter should be liquid and the mozzarella should be stringy.

3. Add the egg, vanilla, and powdered sweetener to the food processor and pulse to combine.

4. Add the melted mozzarella mixture to the food processor and pulse to combine.

5. Remove the dough from the food processor and gently knead it into a ball. When the dough holds its shape, it is ready to be used according to recipe directions.

NUTRITION: 1 SERVING = ¼ RECIPE
CALORIES 307.7 KCAL
CARBOHYDRATE 5.3 G
TOTAL FAT 23.2 G
SATURATED FAT 9.6 G
TRANS FATS 0.5 G
SODIUM 747.5 MG
TOTAL SUGARS 1.4 G
PROTEIN 20.3 G
FIBER 1.3 G

CHICKEN CRUST PIZZA

YIELD: 2 SERVINGS
PREP TIME: 12 MINUTES
COOK TIME: 10 MINUTES

INGREDIENTS

8 ounces (224 g) ground chicken (white or dark meat)

½ cup (50 g) grated Parmesan

¼ cup (7.5 g) crushed pork rinds or (30 g) almond flour

1 large egg

2 tablespoons (7.2 g) Italian seasoning

½ teaspoon chili powder

½ teaspoon salt

¼ teaspoon garlic powder

½ cup (120 ml) sugar-free marinara sauce (e.g., Rao's)

Pizza toppings of choice

INSTRUCTIONS

1. In a food processor, pulse the chicken, Parmesan, pork rinds, and egg to combine.

2. In a small bowl, whisk the Italian seasoning, chili powder, salt, and garlic powder. Then add it to the food processor and pulse to combine.

3. Line the air fryer tray with parchment paper or aluminum foil and grease. Press the crust into a circular disk approximately ½ inch (1.3 cm) thick.

4. Air-fry the crust on the lower rack at 400°F (200°C) for 6 minutes.

5. Remove the crust from the air fryer. Flip it over and add the pizza sauce and toppings.

6. Air-fry the pizza on the upper rack at 450°F (230°C) for 4 minutes, or until the toppings are crisp. Slice it and serve immediately

NUTRITION: 1 SERVING = ½ CRUST
CALORIES 404 KCAL
CARBOHYDRATE 5 G
TOTAL FAT 24.7 G
SATURATED FAT 9 G
TRANS FATS 0.3 G
SODIUM 1271.3 MG
TOTAL SUGARS 0.4 G
PROTEIN 41.4 G
FIBER 0.7 G

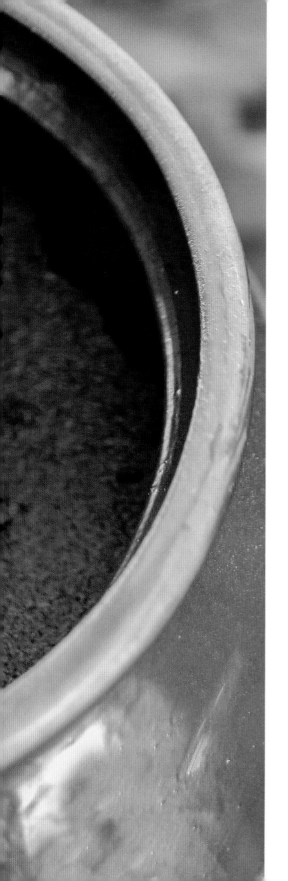

SAUCES & SEASONINGS

BUFFALO SAUCE

YIELD: ½ CUP (120 ML)
PREP TIME: 2 MINUTES
COOK TIME: 3 MINUTES

INGREDIENTS

⅓ cup (80 ml) your favorite
   keto-friendly hot sauce
   (e.g., Frank's)
2 tablespoons (28 g)
   unsalted butter
Dash garlic powder
Dash cayenne pepper

INSTRUCTIONS

1. Combine the hot sauce and butter in a saucepan over medium-low heat. Add the garlic powder and cayenne pepper to taste and whisk to combine.

2. The final consistency will be fairly loose. You can keep the sauce in the fridge in an airtight container for up to a week. Reheat before using it to remelt the butter.

TIP: THIS BUFFALO SAUCE IS A GREAT WAY TO SPICE UP ANY MEAL. WHETHER YOU'RE MAKING A BUFFALO CHICKEN DIP OR TRYING TO ADD A LITTLE KICK TO SOME CAULIFLOWER "WINGS," THIS SIMPLE YET SATISFYING SAUCE DOES THE TRICK. IF YOU'RE A FAN OF IT, MAKE THIS SAUCE IN LARGE BATCHES FOR AN EASY ADDITION TO YOUR FAVORITE MEALS.

NUTRITION: 1 SERVING = ¼ CUP
CALORIES 101.7 KCAL
CARBOHYDRATE 0 G
TOTAL FAT 11.5 G
SATURATED FAT 7.2 G
TRANS FATS 0.5 G
SODIUM 1617.5 MG
TOTAL SUGARS 0 G
PROTEIN 0.1 G
FIBER 0 G

COCONUT CURRY PEANUT SAUCE

YIELD: 2 CUPS (480 ML),
2 SERVINGS
PREP TIME: 8 MINUTES
COOK TIME: 5 MINUTES

INGREDIENTS

1 (14-ounce [329 g]) can unsweetened coconut milk
2 tablespoons (30 g) unsweetened peanut butter or other nut butter
1 tablespoon (8 g) Mae Ploy yellow curry paste
1 tablespoon (15 ml) coconut aminos
1 teaspoon (5 ml) lime juice
½ teaspoon sugar-free fish sauce
Salt, to taste

TIP: THIS SAUCE IS A GREAT ADDITION TO CAULIFLOWER RICE DISHES. IT CAN ALSO BE ADDED TO SHREDDED CHICKEN, A KETO-FRIENDLY VEGETABLE JUMBLE, OR PULLED PORK. THE SAVORY NATURE OF THE FISH SAUCE AND THE NUT BUTTER GIVES IT A HEARTY TASTE, AND THE FRESH LIME JUICE BRIGHTENS THE FLAVOR.

NUTRITION: 1 SERVING = 1 CUP
CALORIES 820.3 KCAL
CARBOHYDRATE 17.8 G
TOTAL FAT 75.9 G
SATURATED FAT 52.5 G
TRANS FATS 0 G
SODIUM 2009.6 MG
TOTAL SUGARS 9.6 G
PROTEIN 10 G
FIBER 4.2 G

INSTRUCTIONS

1. Whisk the coconut milk, nut butter, and curry paste in a saucepan over medium heat to combine. The sauce will begin to emulsify after 5 minutes.

2. Reduce the heat to low and add the coconut aminos, lime juice, fish sauce, and salt. Whisk to combine.

3. This sauce is best consumed fresh, but if stored in an airtight container, it will keep in the fridge for 7 to 10 days.

CHIMICHURRI

YIELD: 2 CUPS (480 ML),
4 SERVINGS
PREP TIME: 12 MINUTES
COOK TIME: 1 MINUTE

INGREDIENTS

1 bunch fresh flat-leaf parsley

½ bunch fresh cilantro

4 to 5 sprigs fresh oregano

1 shallot

4 cloves garlic

1 jalapeño (optional)

¼ cup (60 ml) red wine vinegar

⅓ cup (80 ml) avocado oil

1 teaspoon (6 g) sea salt

¼ teaspoon red pepper flakes

TIP: IN A PINCH, YOU CAN SUB OUT THE CILANTRO AND OREGANO FOR 4 TABLESPOONS (4 G) OF DRIED CILANTRO AND 2 TABLESPOONS (6 G) OF DRIED OREGANO, BUT THE FRESHNESS REALLY BRIGHTENS THE FLAVORS OF THE CHIMICHURRI.

NUTRITION: 1 SERVING = ½ CUP
CALORIES 183.7 KCAL
CARBOHYDRATE 4.4 G
TOTAL FAT 18.3 G
SATURATED FAT 21.9 G
TRANS FATS 0 G
SODIUM 601.7 MG
TOTAL SUGARS 1.3 G
PROTEIN 1 G
FIBER 1 G

INSTRUCTIONS

1. Place 1 packed cup (60 g) of fresh parsley in a food processor.

2. Add ½ packed cup (8 g) of fresh cilantro to the food processor.

3. Add 2 tablespoons (6 g) of oregano to the food processor.

4. Peel the shallot and trim the top and bottom. Roughly chop and add it to the food processor.

5. Crush the garlic cloves with the broad side of a knife and then cut in half. Add to the food processor.

6. If you are using jalapeño, remove the stem and roughly chop it. Add it to the food processor.

7. Add the red wine vinegar, avocado oil, sea salt, and red pepper flakes to the food processor and pulse to combine.

8. This is best consumed fresh, but if stored in an airtight container, it will keep in the fridge for 10 to 12 days.

EVERYTHING SAUCE

YIELD: 1 CUP, 4 SERVINGS

PREP TIME: 4 MINUTES

COOK TIME: N/A

INGREDIENTS

¾ cup (180 g) sour cream

¼ cup (60 g) mayonnaise

¼ cup (60 g) prepared horseradish

2 tablespoons (30 ml) sugar-free ketchup

2 teaspoons (10 ml) apple cider vinegar

1 to 2 teaspoons (5 to 10 ml) your favorite keto-friendly hot sauce (e.g., Primal Kitchen)

½ teaspoon garlic powder

¼ teaspoon salt

INSTRUCTIONS

1. Combine the sour cream, mayonnaise, horseradish, ketchup, vinegar, hot sauce, garlic powder, and salt in a medium-size bowl or in the bowl of your food processor. You can whisk or mix with a fork. The food processor is quick and easy.

2. Stored in an airtight container in the refrigerator, the sauce will keep for 13 to 17 days.

NUTRITION: 1 SERVING = ¼ CUP

CALORIES 390.8 KCAL

CARBOHYDRATE 12.1 G

TOTAL FAT 37.5 G

SATURATED FAT 12 G

TRANS FATS 0.8 G

SODIUM 732.7 MG

TOTAL SUGARS 4.6 G

PROTEIN 2.9 G

FIBER 1.1 G

TIP: ADD MORE HOT SAUCE AND HORSERADISH IF YOU LIKE SPICIER SAUCES. THIS SAUCE IS AN EXCELLENT ADDITION TO JUST ABOUT ANY SAVORY KETO DISH. MAKE LARGE BATCHES AND KEEP IN THE FRIDGE FOR EASY COOKING. IF YOU WANT TO GIVE IT A FRESHER KICK, TRY GRATING FRESH HORSERADISH ROOT AND USING ¼ CUP (30 G) OF THAT. BE WARNED, THIS ROOT VEGETABLE IS HEALTHY FOR YOU, BUT THE RAW HORSERADISH PACKS A WALLOP AND MAY MAKE YOUR NOSE AND EYES RUN IF YOU'RE NOT USED TO IT.

GENERAL TSO SAUCE

YIELD: 1 CUP (185 ML),
2 SERVINGS
PREP TIME: 5 MINUTES +
10 MINUTES RESTING
COOK TIME: 9 MINUTES

INGREDIENTS

2 teaspoons (10 ml) sesame oil

1 teaspoon (5 g) minced garlic

½ teaspoon minced ginger

2 teaspoons (10 ml) chili
    garlic sauce

1 teaspoon (2 g) red pepper flakes

¼ cup (60 ml) chicken broth

¼ cup (60 ml) coconut aminos
    or tamari

¼ teaspoon Chinese five spice blend

3 tablespoons (45 ml) rice vinegar

½ teaspoon peanut butter or other
    nut butter

¼ teaspoon glucomannan

INSTRUCTIONS

1. In a shallow saucepan, heat the sesame oil over medium-low heat. Add the garlic and ginger and cook for about 1 minute, or until fragrant.

2. Stir in the garlic sauce, red pepper flakes, chicken broth, coconut aminos, Chinese five spice blend, and rice vinegar. Bring them to a simmer.

3. Whisk in the nut butter until fully incorporated. It should be a loose sauce. Allow the sauce to simmer for 5 minutes, stirring occasionally, so the flavors can combine.

4. Turn off the heat and add the glucomannan. The sauce will thicken in 10 to 15 minutes.

5. Stored in an airtight container in the refrigerator, the sauce will keep for 12 to 14 days.

NUTRITION: 1 SERVING = ¼ CUP
CALORIES 85.3 KCAL
CARBOHYDRATE 6.3 G
TOTAL FAT 5.2 G
SATURATED FAT 0.8 G
TRANS FATS 0 G
SODIUM 609.6 MG
TOTAL SUGARS 5.7 G
PROTEIN 0.9 G
FIBER 0.1 G

TIP: THERE ARE A LOT OF DELICIOUS THINGS GOING ON IN THIS RECIPE, BUT THE CHINESE FIVE SPICE BLEND IS THE REAL WINNER HERE. YOU SHOULD BE ABLE TO BUY A PREMIXED VERSION (AND I HIGHLY SUGGEST YOU DO FOR CONVENIENCE'S SAKE), BUT IF YOU HAVE A STOCKED SPICE CABINET YOU CAN MAKE YOUR OWN BY GRINDING STAR ANISE PODS, WHOLE CLOVES, A CINNAMON STICK, FENNEL SEEDS, AND SZECHUAN PEPPERCORNS IN A SPICE GRINDER.

0.4 G NET CARBS = 0.5 G CARBOHYDRATES - 0.1 G FIBER

GREEK DRESSING AND MARINADE

YIELD: 1 CUP (240 ML),
4 SERVINGS
PREP TIME: 1 MINUTE
COOK TIME: N/A

INGREDIENTS

½ cup (120 ml) avocado oil

1 large clove garlic, finely minced

2 tablespoons (30 ml) red wine vinegar

2 tablespoons (30 ml) white vinegar

1 tablespoon (15 ml) lemon juice

1 teaspoon (5 ml) Dijon mustard

1 teaspoon (2 g) dried oregano

1 teaspoon (6 g) salt

½ teaspoon dried basil

¼ teaspoon garlic powder

INSTRUCTIONS

1. Combine all the ingredients in an 8-ounce (230 ml) glass jar. They will fit perfectly. Shake vigorously to blend.

2. This sauce will keep in the fridge for 7 to 9 days. Shake it to combine before each use, as it will separate over time.

TIP: THIS IS AN EXCELLENT ADDITION TO ANY LETTUCE WRAP OR IF A DISH IS WANTING. STORE THESE INGREDIENTS IN A GLASS MASON JAR SO THAT YOU CAN SHAKE AND SERVE (OR MARINATE) TO YOUR HEART'S CONTENT.

NUTRITION: 1 SERVING
CALORIES 1233.5 KCAL
CARBOHYDRATE 0.5 G
TOTAL FAT 13.7 G
SATURATED FAT 1.6 G
TRANS FATS 0 G
SODIUM 310.2 MG
TOTAL SUGARS 0.1 G
PROTEIN 0.1 G
FIBER 0.1 G

2.9 G NET CARBS = 3.9 G CARBOHYDRATES - 1 G FIBER

KOREAN GOCHUJANG

YIELD: 1 ⅓ CUP (315.5 ML),
10 SERVINGS
PREP TIME: 5 MINUTES
COOK TIME: N/A

INGREDIENTS

½ cup (120 ml) water

½ cup (50 g) Korean red pepper flakes (gochugaru) or ground red pepper flakes (use a spice grinder)

2 tablespoons (24 g) granulated sugar substitute (e.g., Swerve)

1 tablespoon (15 g) tahini

1 tablespoon (15 ml) rice wine vinegar

1 teaspoon (5 ml) sugar-free fish sauce

1 teaspoon (6 g) salt

INSTRUCTIONS

1. Place all the ingredients in the bowl of a food processor. Pulse to combine into a paste.

2. Scoop out the paste with a spatula and store it in an airtight container in the refrigerator for 3 to 4 weeks.

NUTRITION: 1 SERVING = 2 TABLESPOONS
CALORIES 24.6 KCAL
CARBOHYDRATE 3.9 G
TOTAL FAT 1 G
SATURATED FAT 0.1 G
TRANS FATS 0 G
SODIUM 239.1 MG
TOTAL SUGARS 1.3 G
PROTEIN 1 G
FIBER 1 G

TIP: FOR A SHARPER FLAVOR, TRY SWITCHING OUT 1 TABLESPOON (15 G) OF TAHINI FOR 1 TABLESPOON (17 G) OF MISO. GOCHUJANG HAS ALSO BEEN CALLED KOREAN HOT SAUCE, AND YOU CAN MAKE SOME REALLY TASTY WINGS (CHICKEN OR CAULIFLOWER) WITH THIS RECIPE. BE WARNED, THE SHEER AMOUNT OF RED PEPPER FLAKES MAKES THIS A SUPER SPICY PASTE, SO IF YOU'RE GENEROUSLY ADDING IT TO A RECIPE, MAKE SURE YOU HAVE SOME SORT OF CREAM IN THE DISH TO BALANCE OUT THE HEAT.

LEMON DILL SAUCE

YIELD: 1 CUP, 4 SERVINGS
PREP TIME: 5 MINUTES
COOK TIME: N/A

INGREDIENTS

2 tablespoons (8 g) chopped fresh dill (use the tender tips of the sprig)

⅓ cup (80 g) sour cream

1 tablespoon (14 g) mayonnaise

1 tablespoon (15 ml) lemon juice

2 teaspoons (10 g) Dijon mustard

1 tablespoon (8 g) capers with brine

¼ teaspoon onion powder

Pinch salt

Pinch garlic powder

INSTRUCTIONS

1. Whisk all the ingredients in a bowl to combine until the mixture makes a creamy yellow sauce.

2. Store the sauce in an airtight container in the refrigerator for 7 to 10 days.

NUTRITION: 1 SERVING = ¼ CUP
CALORIES 66.4 KCAL
CARBOHYDRATE 1.5 G
TOTAL FAT 6.5 G
SATURATED FAT 2.4 G
TRANS FATS 0.2 G
SODIUM 285.9 MG
TOTAL SUGARS 0.7 G
PROTEIN 0.7 G
FIBER 0.2 G

TIP: THIS SAUCE IS EXCELLENT WITH FISH OR CHICKEN DISHES. THE DILL ADDS AN EARTHY GREEN FLAVOR WHILE THE SOUR AND ACIDIC NOTES OF THE LEMON JUICE ADD A POP OF TARTNESS. MARINATE MEATS IN IT OR TOSS SOME VEGETABLES IN IT FOR A LIGHTER MEAL.

SESAME SAUCE

YIELD: ½ CUP (120 ML),
4 SERVINGS
PREP TIME: 5 MINUTES +
10 MINUTES RESTING
COOK TIME: 5 MINUTES

INGREDIENTS

2 tablespoons (30 ml) sesame oil

1 teaspoon (5 g) minced fresh garlic

6 tablespoons (90 ml)
coconut aminos

3 tablespoons (45 ml) rice vinegar

2 tablespoons (24 g) brown sugar
substitute (e.g., Swerve Brown)

½ teaspoon red pepper flakes

¼ teaspoon unsweetened fish sauce

¼ teaspoon glucomannan

TIP: VERY SIMILAR TO THE GENERAL TSO SAUCE (PAGE 140), THIS ONE DOESN'T HAVE AS STRONG A KICK. TOSS SOME PRECOOKED MEAT INTO THIS DELICIOUS SAUCE TO LIVEN UP ANY MEAL. SERVE IT WITH THINLY SLICED SCALLIONS CUT AT AN ANGLE AND SESAME SEEDS TO MAKE THIS EASY MEAL SEEM VERY IMPRESSIVE.

NUTRITION: 1 SERVING = 2 TABLESPOONS
CALORIES 87.5 KCAL
CARBOHYDRATE 4.9 G
TOTAL FAT 6.8 G
SATURATED FAT 1 G
TRANS FATS 0 G
SODIUM 498.4 MG
TOTAL SUGARS 4.5 G
PROTEIN 0.3 G
FIBER 0.3 G

INSTRUCTIONS

1. In a shallow saucepan, heat the sesame oil over medium-low heat. Add the garlic and cook for about 1 minute, or until fragrant.

2. Add the coconut aminos, rice vinegar, brown sugar substitute, red pepper flakes, and fish sauce and whisk to combine.

3. Reduce the heat to low and allow the sauce to simmer for 5 minutes, stirring occasionally, for the flavors to combine.

4. Turn off the heat and add the glucomannan. The sauce will thicken in 10 to 15 minutes.

5. Store the sauce in an airtight container in the refrigerator. The sauce will keep for 12 to 14 days.

SWEET CHILI SAUCE

YIELD: ALMOST 1 CUP
(225 ML), 2 SERVINGS
PREP TIME: 4 MINUTES
COOK TIME: 7 MINUTES

INGREDIENTS

4 teaspoons (20 ml) coconut aminos

2 tablespoons (30 ml) rice vinegar

2 tablespoons (30 ml) chili garlic sauce

¼ cup (60 ml) water

2 teaspoons (8 g) granulated sugar substitute (e.g., Swerve)

1 teaspoon (8 g) ground ginger

⅛ teaspoon glucomannan

INSTRUCTIONS

1. In a shallow saucepan over medium-low heat, whisk the coconut aminos, rice vinegar, chili garlic sauce, water, granulated sugar substitute, and ground ginger to combine .

2. Turn off the heat and add the glucomannan; stir to combine. The sauce will thicken in 10 to 15 minutes.

3. Stored in an airtight container in the refrigerator, this sauce will keep for 12 to 14 days.

TIP: THIS SWEET CHILI SAUCE IS AN EXCELLENT DIP FOR DUMPLINGS AND OTHER SAVORY FOODS.

NUTRITION: 1 SERVING = ½ RECIPE
CALORIES 16.2 KCAL
CARBOHYDRATE 2.9 G
TOTAL FAT 0 G
SATURATED FAT 0 G
TRANS FATS 0 G
SODIUM 705.5 MG
TOTAL SUGARS 2 G
PROTEIN 0.1 G
FIBER 0.4 G

TERIYAKI MARINADE AND SAUCE

YIELD: 1 CUP (240 ML),
4 SERVINGS
PREP TIME: 5 MINUTES
COOK TIME: 10 MINUTES

INGREDIENTS

1 teaspoon (5 ml) sesame oil

1 teaspoon (3 g) minced garlic

1 teaspoon (5 g) ginger paste

¾ cup (180 ml) coconut aminos
or tamari

¼ cup (60 ml) water

3 tablespoons (45 ml) apple cider
vinegar or rice vinegar

½ teaspoon fish sauce

1 teaspoon (5 g) golden granulated
sugar substitute (e.g., Swerve)

⅛ teaspoon glucomannan

INSTRUCTIONS

1. In a shallow saucepan, heat the sesame oil over medium-low heat. Add the garlic and ginger and cook for about 1 minute, or until fragrant.

2. Add the coconut aminos, water, vinegar, fish sauce, and sugar substitute. Whisk to combine.

3. Reduce the heat to low and allow the sauce to simmer for 5 minutes, stirring occasionally, for the flavors to combine.

4. Turn off the heat and add the glucomannan; stir to combine. The sauce will thicken in 10 to 15 minutes.

5. Stored in an airtight container in the fridge, this sauce will keep for 3 weeks.

NUTRITION: 1 SERVING = ¼ CUP
CALORIES 60.3 KCAL
CARBOHYDRATE 9.6 G
TOTAL FAT 1.1 G
SATURATED FAT 0.2 G
TRANS FATS 0 G
SODIUM 872.8 MG
TOTAL SUGARS 9.1 G
PROTEIN 0.3 G
FIBER 0 G

TIKKA MASALA SAUCE

YIELD: 2 CUPS (480 ML),
8 SERVINGS
PREP TIME: 5 MINUTES
COOK TIME: 5 MINUTES

INGREDIENTS

1 (13.5-ounce [383 g]) can full-fat coconut milk

¼ cup (60 ml) chicken broth

2 tablespoons (30 g) tomato paste

1 tablespoon (8 g) garam masala

2 teaspoons (10 ml) lemon juice

1 teaspoon (2 g) ground cumin

½ teaspoon ground turmeric

½ teaspoon garlic powder

⅛ teaspoon ground ginger

¼ teaspoon salt

INSTRUCTIONS

1. Combine all the ingredients in a saucepan over medium-low heat, and bring the mixture to a low boil. Whisk to combine and fully incorporate the spices. Let the mixture simmer for 5 minutes.

2. Stored in an airtight container in the refrigerator, this sauce will keep for 10 to 12 days.

NUTRITION: 1 SERVING = ½ CUP
CALORIES 172.3 KCAL
CARBOHYDRATE 4.2 G
TOTAL FAT 16 G
SATURATED FAT 14.6 G
TRANS FATS 0 G
SODIUM 245 MG
TOTAL SUGARS 1.7 G
PROTEIN 1.3 G
FIBER 0.8 G

TIP: MOST TIKKA MASALA SAUCES HAVE A LOT OF ONIONS, PEPPERS, AND GARLIC IN THEM. BECAUSE ONIONS HAVE MORE CARBS THAN WE'D LIKE IN KETO RECIPES, THIS TIKKA MASALA HAS NO SUCH INGREDIENTS. HOWEVER, IF YOU'D LIKE TO ADD A BIT OF FRESHNESS, YOU CAN ROAST RED PEPPERS AND BLEND THEM INTO THE SAUCE FOR ADDED DEPTH OF FLAVOR; SERVE WITH FRESH CILANTRO.

TZATZIKI SAUCE

YIELD: 2 CUPS (480 ML),
8 SERVINGS
PREP TIME: 8 MINUTES
COOK TIME: N/A

INGREDIENTS

1 fresh kirby cucumber
½ cup (120 g) plain Greek yogurt
1 tablespoon (4 g) chopped
   fresh dill
1 teaspoon (5 ml) lemon juice
1 clove garlic, minced
Salt and fresh ground black pepper,
   to taste

TIP: THIS SAUCE IS GREAT FOR LETTUCE
WRAPS AND IS A COOL AND CREAMY ADDITION
TO MOST HOT AND SPICY RECIPES. BECAUSE
TZATZIKI IS A GREEK SAUCE, IT GOES WELL
WITH FOODS COOKED IN THE GREEK MARINADE
(PAGE 141).

NUTRITION: 1 SERVING = ½ CUP
CALORIES 33.6 KCAL
CARBOHYDRATE 3 G
TOTAL FAT 1.9 G
SATURATED FAT 1.1 G
TRANS FATS 0.1 G
SODIUM 20.7 MG
TOTAL SUGARS 2.3 G
PROTEIN 1.4 G
FIBER 0.3 G

INSTRUCTIONS

1. Grate the cucumber with a food processor or hand grater. Leaving the skin on will give the sauce an extra boost of vitamin C, but you can peel it if you prefer.

2. Place the cucumber in a fine-mesh strainer and press out the water. Alternatively, place the cucumber in the center of a clean dish towel and squeeze out as much water as possible.

3. Transfer the cucumber to a medium-size bowl. Add the yogurt, dill, lemon juice, garlic, salt, and pepper and mix with a fork to combine into a creamy sauce.

4. Stored in an airtight container in the refrigerator, the sauce will keep for 10 to 12 days.

0.8 G NET CARBS = 0.8 G CARBOHYDRATES - 0 G FIBER

WONTON DIPPING SAUCE

YIELD: ¼ CUP (30 ML),
1 SERVING
PREP TIME: 6 MINUTES
COOK TIME: N/A

INGREDIENTS

2 tablespoons (30 ml) rice vinegar

1 tablespoon (15 ml) coconut aminos

1 teaspoon (5 g) chili garlic sauce

1 teaspoon chopped scallion

½ teaspoon sesame oil

INSTRUCTIONS

1. Stir all the ingredients in a medium-size bowl to combine.

2. Add more chili garlic sauce to get the sauce to your desired spiciness.

TIP: THIS IS BEST SERVED WITH MORE FRESH SCALLION, THINLY CHOPPED AT AN ANGLE, AND SESAME SEEDS TO REALLY IMPRESS YOUR GUESTS (OR TREAT YOURSELF)! MAKE LARGE BATCHES OF THIS GO-TO DIPPING SAUCE AND STORE IN AN AIRTIGHT CONTAINER IN THE FRIDGE FOR 2 TO 3 WEEKS.

NUTRITION: 1 SERVING = WHOLE RECIPE
CALORIES 10.2 KCAL
CARBOHYDRATE 0.8 G
TOTAL FAT 0.6 G
SATURATED FAT 0.1 G
TRANS FATS 0 G
SODIUM 87.7 MG
TOTAL SUGARS 0.8 G
PROTEIN 0 G
FIBER 0 G

2.6 G NET CARBS = 2.9 G CARBOHYDRATES - 0.3 G FIBER

YOGURT MINT CHUTNEY

YIELD: 2 ¼ CUP (270 ML),
4 SERVINGS
PREP TIME: 2 MINUTES
COOK TIME: N/A

INGREDIENTS

½ cup (120 g) plain Greek yogurt
   (or ¼ cup [60 g] Greek yogurt
   and ¼ cup [60 g] sour cream)
1 cup (90 g) chopped fresh
   mint leaves
½ cup (8 g) chopped fresh
   cilantro leaves
1 jalapeño, sliced
3 tablespoons (45 ml) lemon juice
2 teaspoons grated fresh ginger or
   ginger paste
1 clove garlic, roughly chopped
½ teaspoon salt
½ teaspoon sugar substitute
   (optional)

INSTRUCTIONS

1. Pulse all the ingredients in a food processor
   to combine.

2. Stored in an airtight container in the refrigerator,
   the sauce will keep for 10 to 12 days.

NUTRITION: 1 SERVING = 1 HEAPING CUP
CALORIES 35.3 KCAL
CARBOHYDRATE 2.9 G
TOTAL FAT 2 G
SATURATED FAT 1.1 G
TRANS FATS 0.1 G
SODIUM 317.8 MG
TOTAL SUGARS 2.2 G
PROTEIN 1.6 G
FIBER 0.3 G

TIP: IT'S A GOOD IDEA TO REMOVE THE RIBS AND SEEDS OF THE
JALAPEÑO, BUT IF YOU WANT TO GIVE THIS CHUTNEY A LITTLE EXTRA
KICK, LEAVE SOME OF THE SEEDS, AS THAT'S WHERE JALAPEÑOS
STORE THEIR SPICE.

CRUMB COATING

YIELD: 4 ¼ CUPS (81 G),
8 SERVINGS
PREP TIME: 5 MINUTES
COOK TIME: N/A

INGREDIENTS

4 cups or 2 ounces (56 g) crushed pork rinds

¼ cup (25 g) grated Parmesan

1 teaspoon (6 g) salt

2 teaspoons seasoning based upon intended use

INSTRUCTIONS

1. Whisk all the ingredients in a small bowl to combine.

2. Store excess crumb coating in an airtight container in the fridge. It will keep for 10 to 14 days.

TIP: THIS RECIPE GETS USED *A LOT* IN THIS BOOK, AND FOR GOOD REASON. IT'S EASY AND DELICIOUS. IF THE PORK RINDS ARE ALREADY CRUSHED, THEN YOU JUST MIX WITH A SPOON. OR YOU CAN PURCHASE WHOLE PORK RINDS AND CRUSH THEM IN THE BAG. PULVERIZING PORK RINDS IN A FOOD PROCESSOR IS ALSO AN OPTION.

NUTRITION: 1 SERVING = HEAPING ½ CUP
CALORIES 425 KCAL
CARBOHYDRATE 3.5 G
TOTAL FAT 27 G
SATURATED FAT 9.8 G
TRANS FATS 0.2 G
SODIUM 3568.7 MG
TOTAL SUGARS 0 G
PROTEIN 43.1 G
FIBER 0 G

ADOBO SEASONING

YIELD: ¼ CUP, 10 SERVINGS
PREP TIME: 4 MINUTES
COOK TIME: N/A

INGREDIENTS

2 tablespoons (34 g) salt

1 tablespoon (9 g) garlic powder

1 tablespoon (9 g) paprika

2 teaspoons (4 g) ground black pepper

1 teaspoon (2 g) onion powder

1 teaspoon (2 g) dried oregano

1 teaspoon (3 g) chili powder

INSTRUCTIONS

1. Whisk all the spices to a small bowl to combine.

2. Store the seasoning in an airtight container or glass jar.

NUTRITION: 1 SERVING
CALORIES 8.1 KCAL
CARBOHYDRATE 1.8 G
TOTAL FAT 0.2 G
SATURATED FAT 0 G
TRANS FATS 0 G
SODIUM 1423.6 MG
TOTAL SUGARS 0.1 G
PROTEIN 0.4 G
FIBER 0.6 G

CAJUN SEASONING

YIELD: ¼ CUP, 10 SERVINGS
PREP TIME: 5 MINUTES
COOK TIME: N/A

INGREDIENTS

2 tablespoons (34 g) salt

2 tablespoons (18 g) paprika

2 tablespoons (18 g) garlic powder

1 tablespoon (3 g) dried oregano

2 teaspoons (4 g) onion powder

1 teaspoon (2 g) cayenne pepper

1 teaspoon (2 g) ground
   white pepper

1 teaspoon (1 g) dried thyme

1 teaspoon (2 g) red pepper flakes

INSTRUCTIONS

1. Whisk all the spices in a small bowl to combine.

2. Store the seasoning in an airtight container or glass jar.

NUTRITION: 1 SERVING
CALORIES 14 KCAL
CARBOHYDRATE 3 G
TOTAL FAT 0.3 G
SATURATED FAT 0.1 G
TRANS FATS 0 G
SODIUM 1417.3 MG
TOTAL SUGARS 0.3 G
PROTEIN 0.6 G
FIBER 1 G

RANCH SEASONING

YIELD: ¼ CUP, 10 SERVINGS
PREP TIME: 5 MINUTES
COOK TIME: N/A

INGREDIENTS

2 tablespoons (3 g) dried parsley

2 tablespoons (3 g) dried dill

2 teaspoons (2 g) dried chives

1 teaspoon (3 g) garlic powder

1 teaspoon (2 g) onion powder

½ teaspoon dried oregano

½ teaspoon dried basil

INSTRUCTIONS

1. Whisk all the spices in a small bowl to combine.

2. Store the seasoning in an airtight container or glass jar.

NUTRITION: 1 SERVING
CALORIES 4.6 KCAL
CARBOHYDRATE 1 G
TOTAL FAT 0.1 G
SATURATED FAT 0 G
TRANS FATS 0 G
SODIUM 3.1 MG
TOTAL SUGARS 0.3 G
PROTEIN 0.3 G
FIBER 0.3 G

INDEX